mormonism
EXPLAINED

mormonism EXPLaineD

What Latter-day Saints Teach and Practice

ANDREW JACKSON

CROSSWAY BOOKS
WHEATON, ILLINOIS

Mormonism Explained: What Latter-day Saints Teach and Practice

Published by Crossway Books
          a publishing ministry of Good News Publishers
          1300 Crescent Street
          Wheaton, Illinois 60187

Design and typesetting by Lakeside Design Plus
Cover design: Jon McGrath
Cover Illustration: iStock Photo
First printing 2008
Printed in the United States of America

Library of Congress Cataloging-in-Publication Data
Jackson, Andrew, 1953–
        Mormonism explained : what Latter-day Saints teach and practice /
Andrew Jackson.
              p. cm.
        Includes bibliographical references and index.
        ISBN 978-1-58134-935-1 (tpb)
        1. Church of Jesus Christ of Latter-day Saints—Doctrines. 2. Mormon
Church—Doctrines. 3. Church of Jesus Christ of Latter-day Saints—
Customs and practices. 4. Mormon Church—Customs and practices. I. Title.
BX8635.3.J33 2008
230'.93—dc22
                                                                2007042038

CH	18	17	16	15	14	13	12	11	10	09	08
12	11	10	9	8	7	6	5	4	3	2	1

To the Family I Love Beyond Words

Barbara, Rachael, Luke, and Sarah Grace

contents

INTRODUCTION

y goal in writing *Mormonism Explained* was to present a concise and thorough introduction to what Latter-day Saints (LDS) officially teach and practice today primarily for the broad Christian audience, although I also wrote it for interested non-Christians and Mormons.

Diversity within Mormonism

Unfortunately, many Christians have had a tendency to stereotype Mormons and see them as all being the same. This is not true. The fact is, Mormonism contains quite a bit of diversity, and several streams of Mormon thinking and opinions exist today, although they are all still under the careful oversight of the LDS Church hierarchy.

There are Latter-day Saints who swim within the theological waters of the more traditional Mormonism represented by systematic theologian Bruce McConkie, other Mormons who embrace the progressive Mormon scholarship of Brigham Young University professors such as Dr. Stephen Robinson and Dr. Robert Millet, and then many—if not most—Mormons who were born into LDS families, live their daily lives inside the culture and world of Mormonism, and really do not think a lot about the intricacies and theological validity of LDS teaching and practices. They seem content and happy being Mormon, and exert little energy in thinking through and evaluating the details or truthfulness of their faith.

My Mormon Qualifications

What are my qualifications to write a book on Mormonism? Many Latter-day Saints—although not all—will dismiss my book simply because I am not Mormon and have never been a Mormon. They seem to believe that only Mormons should have the privilege of writing about what the LDS teach and practice. For many Mormons, any "outsider" is seemingly suspect, if not outright labeled a deceiving enemy of their claimed restored gospel. Being called a religious bigot or Mormon-hater is not always the most pleasant experience. I must admit that I do not fully understand this Mormon mind-set, for it strongly smacks of an unhealthy martyr complex, a form of anti-intellectualism, and a fear of scholarly evaluation or critique, whether by Mormons, non-Mormons, or ex-Mormons.

Although I am not Mormon, I did not write this book in complete ignorance, in distant abstraction, or from a socially or theologically detached position. I have lived among and interacted with Mormons and Mormon culture for over a decade now as I serve as a pastor in a church in downtown Mesa, Arizona, which is one block down from the historic Arizona temple. As many of you know, the city of Mesa was pioneered and founded by the Mormons in January 1878. In fact, the large grassy park that separates our church campus and the Arizona temple is named "Pioneer Park," memorializing the early Mormon pioneers of Mesa. As a result of living in the East Valley of the Phoenix area, I have many Mormon neighbors, acquaintances, and friends.

My Research Challenges

In writing this book, I experienced several research challenges. Probably the greatest one was determining what written, online, and individual Mormon resources I should primarily use to determine what Latter-day Saints actually teach and practice. Following is a short description of my experience in engaging in this Mormon resource search.

First, it became clear early on that average Mormons—not unlike many Christians—are simply not able to accurately and thoroughly provide a systematic explanation of their beliefs. Second, young Mormon missionaries, part of the landscape in Phoenix's East Valley, are also actually quite theologically uninformed in the LDS faith, as Dr. Stephen Robinson himself attests:

> The LDS missionaries receive very little formal training before going out to proselytize. They are almost literally babes in the woods. In fact, Mormon missionaries might be among the least knowledgeable members in a congregation. Actually such elementary understanding as most missionaries have, while it meets the needs of LDS proselytizing by bearing simple testimony, hardly constitutes a sophisticated guide to LDS doctrinal specifics. And to top it off, Mormon missionaries frequently say a lot more than they actually really know.[1]

Third, Mormons seem to portray a pride in the fact that their church leaders are volunteers and are not paid. And this is true, but you quickly discover that the leaders are also not biblically or theologically trained, and I did not find them to be a collective informed resource for my book either. Again, Dr. Robinson is quite candid about describing the lack of formal biblical and theological training by today's LDS Church leadership.[2]

Yet I did find some of the unofficial yet informed LDS apologists and their Web sites somewhat helpful, especially some of the members of the Foundation for Apologetic Information and Research (FAIR), who graciously engaged in periodic e-mail interactions with me. I did find it frustrating at times that Mormon apologists and others would want to passionately tell me what the LDS Church really teaches and practices, but then be very quick to qualify that they in no way spoke for the LDS Church.

In the end, I must say that for someone attempting to write a well-researched book on the teaching and practices of the LDS Church, the discovery that most average Mormons, Mormon missionaries, and Mormon leaders were not quality resources of credible information and insight provided quite a research challenge.

What Is Official Mormonism?

So how does a researcher and writer actually discover the official teaching and practices of the LDS Church? In my case, I decided to lean on the following statements made by Dr. Stephen Robinson and Dr. Robert Millet:

> The only binding sources of doctrine for Latter-day Saints are the Standard Works of the church: the Bible, Book of Mormon, Doctrine and Covenants, and the Pearl of Great Price. The only official interpretations and applications of these doctrinal sources are those that come to the church over the signatures of the First Presidency or the Quorum of the Twelve Apostles (collectively). All the rest is commentary.[3]

> The declaration, clarification, and interpretation of doctrine for the church as a whole rest with the presiding councils of the church, the First Presidency and the Quorum of the Twelve Apostles.[4]

As I explain in more detail in chapter 5, Mormon teaching and practices today are based primarily in the continual divine revelations and interpretations of the LDS President and Prophet and other top apostles, and only secondarily in Mormonism's four written scriptural books that consist of the Bible (King James Version only), *Book of Mormon*, *Doctrine and Covenants*, and *Pearl of Great Price*.[5] In Mormonism, all contemporary experiences of revelation and interpretation by the LDS President and Prophet surpass all past written records of revelation in authority, including the Bible.[6] In the Mormon mind, what God communicated in the past—even if identified as Holy Scripture—is always secondary to what God is saying to ordained Mormon apostles and prophets today.[7]

What about the Bible? Although Mormonism values the Bible, the LDS Church also states that the Bible has been corrupted, contains errors, and is missing many plain and precious truths concerning salvation.[8] As a result, within Mormonism the Bible is functionally subordinate and subject to clarification and revision by the *Book of Mormon*, *Doctrine and Covenants*, and *Pearl of Great Price*.

My Primary Mormon and Non-Mormon Resources

In writing my book, I had to make a major decision concerning what primary Mormon resources I would use. As you can see from the quotations and notes, I drew extensively—although not exclusively—from the writings of Mormon founders Joseph Smith and Brigham Young, official LDS Web sites,[9] the manuals and curriculum produced and distributed by the LDS Church Educational System,[10] the *Encyclopedia of Mormonism*,[11] Richard Lyman Bushman's biography *Joseph Smith: Rough Stone Rolling*, traditional systematic theologian Bruce McConkie's book *Mormon Doctrine*, and the books of progressive Brigham

Young University professors Dr. Stephen Robinson and Dr. Robert Millet.

The primary non-Mormon books that I gleaned from were Dr. Craig Blomberg's writing in *How Wide the Divide? A Mormon & an Evangelical in Conversation,* the book *The New Mormon Challenge: Responding to the Latest Defenses of a Fast-Growing Movement,* and Richard and Joan Ostling's well-researched book *Mormon America: The Power and the Promise.*

The Origins
of Mormonism

one

JOSEPH SMITH: THE RESTORER OF THE TRUE GOSPEL?

Mormonism originates solely from the early-nineteenth-century visions and revelations of Joseph Smith, the first President and Prophet of the Church of Jesus Christ of Latter-day Saints. In this most fundamental fact, Latter-day Saints present no argument or dispute. As the tenth Mormon President and Prophet, Joseph Fielding Smith, affirms with prophetic conviction: "Mormonism must stand or fall on the story of Joseph Smith." Put simply, without Joseph Smith, there would be no such faith known as Mormonism today.[1]

Joseph Smith's Early Years (1805–1820)

Early Mormon history unfolded in the cold winters of the northeastern United States, in such places as Massachusetts, New Hampshire, Vermont, and western New York.[2] In Sharon, Vermont, Joseph Smith Jr. was born on December 23, 1805, to the poor farming family of Joseph and Lucy Mack Smith. The Smith family moved numerous times during Joseph's early teen years, seeking good farmland and a stable living. From 1811 to 1816, they seemed to be constantly on the move, looking for a place they could call home.

In 1816, Joseph Smith Sr. once again packed up his eight children and moved his family to neighboring Palmyra and Manchester Townships located in Ontario County, New York,[3] where they purchased a hundred acres of land and built a small log home. In 1820, in a wooded grove near this log home, Mormonism officially began with Joseph's Smith's "First Vision" experience at the very young age of fourteen.[4]

Joseph Smith's First Vision (1820)

In the early nineteenth century, the western frontier region of New York State experienced zealous Christian revivals and camp meetings common to America's Second Great Awakening.[5] New York earned its reputation of being a "burned-over religious district" as the result of out-of-control spiritual wildfires. It was a region swarming with itinerant flamboyant preachers.[6]

Along with mass personal conversions, ecstatic experiences of encountering God, and transcendent visions, another general characteristic of America's Second Great Awakening was the desire by many Christian groups to break away from historical, creed-centered Christianity in the pursuit of "restoring" the pure practice of the New Testament church. Their efforts were often fueled by homespun theology and end-time predictions of the imminent return of Jesus Christ and his millennial reign.

Early Mormonism reflected many of the common Christian trends of the times: having an authoritarian prophetic leader and being noncreedal,[7] staunchly Arminian,[8] fervently restorationist,[9] evangelistically driven, end-time-focused, and characterized by isolated communal living.[10]

Which Christian Church Is True?

Unfortunately, denominational rivalries and theological debates were rabid in western New York, especially among the Presbyterians, Methodists, and Baptists.[11] As an impressionable, immature boy, Joseph Smith struggled deeply with the question concerning what church denomination was really the true one. During this troubled season, he wrote that he was determined to act on the familiar Bible passage of James 1:5: "If any of you lacks wisdom, let him ask God, who gives generously to all without reproach, and it will be given him."[12]

The First Vision of Joseph Smith

On a clear spring morning in 1820, fourteen-year-old Joseph Smith[13] secluded himself in a grove of trees near his family's log home and knelt in desperation before God, requesting to receive divine wisdom concerning which Christian denomination was the true church.[14] While he was battling the dark power of Satan,[15] two distinct personages with tangible bodies appeared in indescribable glorious light.[16] They were identified as Father God and Jesus Christ. This was the first of numerous divine visitations claimed by Joseph Smith throughout his lifetime, including Moroni, John the Baptist, the apostles Peter, James, and John, Jesus, Moses, Elijah, and many angels.[17]

It was during this momentous encounter that Jesus Christ reportedly exhorted the young boy not to join any Christian church because they were all corrupt and all their doctrinal creeds were simply teachings of men and an abomination to God.

The Cornerstone of the LDS Faith

For Mormons, Joseph Smith's First Vision marks the beginning of the restoration of the true authority-endowed church of Jesus Christ back to the earth. Although there are numerous separate written accounts concerning the actual details of Smith's heavenly vision,[18] the LDS Church has officially canonized only the 1838 version that Joseph Smith wrote eighteen years after his apparent experience. This official version is published today in the *Pearl of Great Price*, one of the four Standard Works of Mormonism.[19] The First Vision story is the cornerstone on which the LDS Church is built. An official LDS Web site says:

> Joseph Smith's First Vision stands today as the greatest event in world history since the birth, ministry, and resurrection of Jesus Christ. After centuries of darkness, the Lord opened the heavens to reveal His word and restore His Church through His chosen prophet.[20]

Mormon President and Prophet Gordon B. Hinckley is even more precise in this General Conference statement:

> Our entire case, as members of The Church of Jesus Christ of Latter-day Saints, rests on the validity of this glorious First Vision. Nothing on which we base our doctrine, nothing we teach, nothing we live by, is of greater importance than this initial declaration.[21]

It is Joseph Smith's First Vision story that Mormon missionaries are trained with scripted precision to tell potential converts.[22]

Joseph Smith's Teen Years (1820–1823)

The three years or so following Joseph Smith's First Vision were uneventful. From the age of fourteen to seventeen, Smith experienced no further visitations, revelations, or visions, yet he did fall into significant temptation and error. Here is his personal confession:

> I was left to all kinds of temptations; and, mingling with all kinds of society, I frequently fell into many foolish errors, and displayed the weakness of youth, and the foibles of human nature; which, I am sorry to say, led me into diverse temptations, offensive in the sight of God.[23]

For Mormons, Joseph Smith's wayward teen years are chalked up as a time for the young man "to grow, mature, gain experience, and receive further nurturing."[24]

One of the more startling bits of historical information, however, is that for years following Joseph Smith's First Vision, he and his father were actively engaged in the practice of magic and divination in their desire to discover hidden treasure. They used seer stones and divining rods as instruments. Joseph Smith Jr. found two stones in 1822 and used them to see "invisible things." He gained a reputation as someone who could use these seer stones to find lost property, buried money, and other hidden things.[25] As we will see later, Joseph Smith even used seer stones to translate the *Book of Mormon*.[26] LDS historian Richard Lyman Bushman writes:

> Joseph Jr. never repudiated the stones or denied their power to find treasure. Remnants of the magical culture stayed with him to the end. But after 1823, he began to orient himself away from treasure and toward translation.[27]

In 1888, the fifth Mormon President and Prophet, Wilford Woodruff, actually consecrated one of Smith's seer stones on a temple altar in Manti, Utah.[28]

Another major chapter in the early origins of Mormonism opens with Joseph Smith's visits by an exalted angel named Moroni (pronounced mor-**ohn**-ı).

Joseph Smith's Moroni Visitations (1823–1827)

On September 21, 1823, approximately three years after his First Vision, seventeen-year-old Joseph Smith reported that he experienced three visits in one night from the angel Moroni.[29] Moroni's visitation provided him with information about the existence and location of the *Book of Mormon*.

According to Joseph Smith, while he was praying late at night, a very bright light appeared in his room and a heavenly personage wearing a loose white robe stood before him in midair. The exalted being announced that he was Moroni, a special messenger sent from God. Moroni declared to the young Smith that God had an unprecedented salvation ministry for him to perform worldwide.

Immediately, Moroni unveiled the millennial-long secret of a sacred book—today called the *Book of Mormon*—hidden inside a stone box that was buried on Hill Cumorah only a few miles away.[30] This book was written on thin gold plates six inches wide and bound with three large rings.[31]

Moroni also told Smith that inside the stone box with the gold book was the Urim and Thummim, obscure objects mentioned in the Old Testament.[32] The Urim and Thummim, composed of two special seer stones attached on silver bows that fastened to a breastplate, were to be used to translate the contents of the gold book from its original language of "Reformed Egyptian"[33] to King James English.

Joseph Smith describes the Urim and Thummim this way:

> With the records was found a curious instrument, which the ancients called "Urim and Thummim," which consisted of two transparent stones set in the rim of a bow fastened to a breast plate. Through the medium of the Urim and Thummim I translated the record by the gift and power of God.[34]

It is revealing that no such language as Reformed Egyptian is known or confirmed by any Egyptologist.

Joseph Smith Sees the Book of Mormon

The next day—September 22, 1823—the angel Moroni once again appeared to Joseph Smith. Moroni told Smith to go to Hill Cumorah,[35] where the gold book—the *Book of Mormon*—was buried. When he arrived, he rapidly found the buried stone box and pried it open, seeing the gold book and the seer stones. When Smith attempted to remove them from the stone box, however, he experienced a severe physical shock. Moroni quickly rebuked him and told him that he required another four years of spiritual preparation before he would be ready to take possession of them at the age of twenty-one.[36]

Who Was Moroni?

It is within the story of the *Book of Mormon* that Moroni's personal identification is discovered. The *Book of Mormon* tells the narration of two peoples—the Nephites and the Lamanites—who lived on the American continent between approximately 600 BC and AD 400. The earliest family members of the Nephites and the Lamanites had emigrated from Israel to America.

Moroni was the eldest son of Mormon, a Nephite prophet and military commander-in-chief, after whom the *Book of Mormon* is named. Moroni served under Mormon in the final great battle between the initially good Nephites and the bad Lamanites in AD 421.

Prior to this final war, Mormon gave the gold book to Moroni and commanded him to preserve it for future generations. During this war, the Lamanites killed Mormon and all the other Nephites, while Moroni escaped and went into hiding. Before Moroni died, he added final contents to the *Book of Mormon* and buried it on Hill Cumorah, where it remained untouched for fourteen hundred years.

Moroni met Joseph Smith on Hill Cumorah each year on September 22 from 1823 to 1827. During these four years, Joseph Smith received intense tutoring and preparation from Moroni in order that he would be found worthy to receive the gold book. Joseph Smith wrote about his experience:

> Accordingly, as I had been commanded, I went at the end of each year, and at each time I found the same messenger there, and received instruction and intelligence from him at each of our interviews, respecting what the Lord was going to do, and how and in what manner His kingdom was to be conducted in the last days.[37]

Today, an LDS monument stands on Hill Cumorah in New York. A ten-foot bronze figure of Moroni is stationed on top of a twenty-five-foot shaft of white granite. The figure is pointing toward heaven with his right hand and holding a replica of the gold *Book of Mormon* tablets in his left hand.[38] The image of the angel Moroni blowing a trumpet also stands atop many LDS temples, which Mormons see as a fulfillment of Revelation 14:6:

> Then I saw another angel flying directly overhead, with an eternal gospel to proclaim to those who dwell on earth, to every nation and tribe and language and people.

More Treasure-Hunting in Pennsylvania

Even during Joseph Smith's intense tutoring times with Moroni, he and his father gained a strong local reputation for using divination to hunt for treasure. In October 1825, approximately two years into his Moroni preparation years, Joseph Jr. was hired by Josiah Stowell to help him search for hidden treasure in an old Spanish silver mine located near Harmony Township,

Pennsylvania. While in Pennsylvania, these treasure hunters boarded with the Isaac Hale family. After approximately one month of searching for treasure, they had no success and abandoned the exploration.

Although LDS authorities have often denied Joseph Smith's treasure-hunting, he was found guilty of disorderly conduct and treasure-hunting through the use of divination on March 20, 1826, in Bainbridge, New York.[39]

Joseph Smith Marries Emma Hale

While Joseph Smith was boarding at Isaac Hale's Pennsylvania home, he fell in love with Isaac's daughter Emma. When Isaac Hale strongly disapproved of his daughter's marrying Smith, he and Emma ran off and eloped. They were married on January 18, 1827.

Immediately after their marriage, Joseph and Emma moved to the Smiths' family home in Manchester, New York, where they farmed with Joseph Sr. throughout the summer of 1827.

Late one night in the fall of 1827, Moroni again appeared to Joseph Smith, declaring that he was now ready before God to receive the gold book. On the early morning of September 22, Moroni led the twenty-one-year-old Smith to Hill Cumorah and gave him the gold tablets and Urim and Thummim.[40] After hiding the gold tablets in a hollowed-out birch log, Joseph Smith would find that from then on, his life would be preoccupied with protecting and translating them.

Joseph Smith in Pennsylvania (1827–1830)

Rather abruptly, Joseph Smith decided to permanently move to Pennsylvania, where he would end up living for over two and a half years, from December 1827 to August 1830. Joseph Smith was apparently motivated to rush to Pennsylvania because he thought many people were trying to steal the gold book from him, and so he decided to take Emma and move back to her father's home in Pennsylvania. Hiding the gold book in a barrel of beans in the back of his wagon, Joseph and Emma Smith rode out of town toward Harmony on a wintry day in December 1827.

The Translation of the Book of Mormon

Joseph and Emma Smith stayed temporarily with the Hale family before purchasing a small two-story home, where Smith began his translation of the *Book of Mormon* sometime between December 1827 and February 1828.[41] Although the Bible records no such spiritual gift as translation,[42] Joseph Smith claimed to possess the spirit of revelation and translation.

Although the detailed process of how Joseph Smith translated the *Book of Mormon* is not fully known, it seems clear that he would stare at the seer stone or the Urim and Thummim through which he would see words, similar to seeing lost objects or treasure, and dictate them to a secretary, who would write them down.[43] Smith would apparently stare for hours through egg-shaped seer stones located at the bottom of a hat, and dictate—by the gift and power of God—English characters he saw to his scribes, Martin Harris and Oliver Cowdery.[44] This is how Daniel Peterson, a professor at Brigham Young University, describes Joseph Smith's so-called translation process of the *Book of Mormon*:

> We know that Joseph didn't translate the way that a scholar would translate. He didn't know Egyptian. There were a couple of means that were prepared for this. One was he used an instrument that was found with the plates that was called the Urim and Thummim. This is a kind of a divinatory device that goes back into Old Testament times. Actually most of the translation was done using something called a seer stone. He would put the stone in the bottom of a hat, presumably to exclude

surrounding light. And then he would put his face into the hat. It's a kind of a strange image for us.[45]

It is also said that Joseph Smith seemed to be in the grip of creative forces that caused him to dictate in rapid fashion, with pages pouring out of his mind like *Messiah* from the pen of George Frideric Handel. With this understanding, the *Book of Mormon* is really more a revelation than a translation.[46] LDS historian Richard Lyman Bushman succinctly summarizes Smith's translation powers and process this way:

> Neither his education nor his Christian upbringing prepared Joseph to translate a book, but the magic culture may have. Treasure-seeking taught Joseph to look for the unseen in a stone. His first reaction when he brought home the Urim and Thummim was delight with its divining powers. "I can see any thing," he told his friend Joseph Knight. He knew from working with his own seer stone what to expect from the Urim and Thummim: he would "see." Practice with his scrying stones carried over to translation of the gold plates. In fact, as work on the *Book of Mormon* proceeded, a seer stone took the place of the Urim and Thummim as an aid in the work, blending magic with inspired translation.[47]

The *Book of Mormon* translation was finished between April and June of 1829, approximately sixteen to seventeen months after Smith had started. Immediately following the completion of the translation, Smith showed it to eleven people. But we know that six of these witnesses—including key early Mormon leaders Martin Harris, Oliver Cowdery, and David Whitmer—would eventually leave the LDS Church.[48] Joseph Smith reported that he returned the original gold plates to Moroni, who apparently took them into heaven. On June 11, 1829, Joseph Smith was granted a copyright and began to plan the publication of the *Book of Mormon*.[49]

As Smith was translating the *Book of Mormon*, he was also engaged in far-out interpretations of the Bible. In April 1829, while in Pennsylvania, he claimed to receive a revelation that the apostle John was still living,[50] based on John 21:20–23:

> Peter turned and saw the disciple whom Jesus loved following them, the one who had been reclining at table close to him and had said, "Lord, who is it that is going to betray you?" When Peter saw him, he said to Jesus, "Lord, what about this man?" Jesus said to him, "If it is my will that he remain until I come, what is that to you? You follow me!" So the saying spread abroad among the brothers that this disciple was not to die; yet Jesus did not say to him that he was not to die, but, "If it is my will that he remain until I come, what is that to you?"

More Supernatural Visitations and the Mormon Priesthoods

The Joseph Smith story continues with more supernatural visitations from John the Baptist and the apostles Peter, James, and John.[51] The Mormon Church claims that through these heavenly visits it alone possesses the God-given authority of the Aaronic and Melchizedek Priesthoods to act as the only lawful agent in building the kingdom of God on earth.[52]

On May 15, 1829, Joseph Smith and Oliver Cowdery went into the woods to pray along Pennsylvania's Susquehanna River. While they were engaged in prayer together, John the Baptist—acting under the authority of the apostles Peter, James, and John—descended from heaven, laid his hands on them, and authoritatively imparted the priesthood of Aaron.[53] John the Baptist then directed Smith and Cowdery to baptize each other in the river. They emerged out of the water full of the Holy Ghost, prophesying, and experiencing a new enlightenment to the true meaning of the Bible.

As the story was told—although the exact time is unclear—shortly after the visitation by John the Baptist, Smith and Cowdery were also visited by the apostles Peter, James, and John, who ordained them into the advanced Melchizedek Priesthood and gave them the keys of apostleship.[54]

Although Joseph Smith and Oliver Cowdery had received the authority of the Aaronic and Melchizedek Priesthoods, they had not as yet received from Elijah the keys of sealing, binding, and loosing, relating to the ability to perform ordinances for the living and the dead.[55] This anointing was restored by Elijah when he apparently appeared to them during the dedication of the Kirtland, Ohio, temple in 1836.

The Publication of the Book of Mormon

Joseph Smith chose twenty-three-year-old printer Egert Grandin of Palmyra, New York, to publish the first edition of the *Book of Mormon* manuscript. Oliver Cowdery and Hyrum Smith supervised the printing, while Joseph Smith continued to live in Pennsylvania. The pages of the *Book of Mormon* were gradually taken to Grandin over several months. Since the translation manuscript was delivered with rough formatting, Grandin's typesetter, John Gilbert, added the punctuation and paragraphing.[56] On August 17, 1829, five thousand copies of the *Book of Mormon* were printed, costing approximately $3,000. It went on sale on April 6, 1830, for $1.25 per copy.

The First Mormon Church

Ten years after his First Vision, and only a few weeks after the publication of the *Book of Mormon,* Joseph Smith—now twenty-four years old—officially organized the first Mormon church on April 6, 1830, based in the little farmhouse of Peter Whitmer Sr. in Fayette, New York.[57] Mormons believe that April 6 is the birthday of Jesus Christ himself and thus connect the incarnation of Jesus Christ with the birth of the first Mormon church.[58]

Approximately forty to fifty people gathered for the official ceremony, and Smith appointed official organizers to meet New York's legal requirements for incorporating a religious society. Joseph Smith and Oliver Cowdery ordained each other to be the church's first elders. The new kingdom of God on earth was named the *Church of Christ*.

During the first general conference of the Mormon Church on June 9, 1830,[59] Joseph Smith received a revelation declaring himself the Mormons' primary "seer, translator, prophet, and apostle of Jesus Christ."[60] In this revelation, the Lord instructed the members of the newborn church to receive Joseph's words as if they were spoken by God himself.[61] Joseph Smith made it very clear from the beginning of the LDS Church that he alone held the keys of the mysteries of the kingdom of God on earth, and that only his utterances carried God's authority for the Latter-day Saints.[62] To this day, the ultimate authority of the Mormon Church is only and exclusively embodied in its residing President and Prophet.

Although Joseph Smith continued to live in Pennsylvania, the proactive exertion of his claims of ultimate authority and revelations from God would lead a small group of Mormons westward into lands unknown—and into a future normally found only in fairy tales.

JOSEPH SMITH'S Mormons MOVE WEST

Under the prophetic leadership of Joseph Smith, the Mormons became a movement—literally. For fourteen years, from 1830 to 1844, Joseph Smith led the Mormons by divine revelations from New York westward to Ohio, Missouri, and finally Illinois, where he was murdered on June 27, 1844, at the young age of thirty-eight.

During these westward migration years, many new Joseph Smith visions and revelations were recorded and canonized in the *Doctrine and Covenants*, which serves today as Mormon-authorized Scripture for LDS teaching and practices.

The Mormons moved westward in the United States, driven by a prophetic passion to locate and establish the holy city of Zion, the final gathering place, and the New Jerusalem of God.[1] Their heads were filled with the vision of Zion descending from heaven as seen in Revelation 21:1–2:

Then I saw a new heaven and a new earth, for the first heaven and the first earth had passed away, and the sea was no more. And I saw the holy city, new Jerusalem, coming down out of heaven from God, prepared as a bride adorned for her husband.

Zion in America

These early Mormons believed that the New Jerusalem would be found in America,[2] and they longed for America's Zion. It would be a place of rest, protection, and freedom from anti-Mormon persecution and life's tribulations.[3] Following the publication of the *Book of Mormon* on August 17, 1829, and the first organized Mormon church on April 6, 1830, Joseph Smith was ready to lead the Mormons toward the future of Zion through the spirit of revelation as their leading prophet and apostle.[4]

While still living in Pennsylvania, Joseph Smith immediately declared the Mormon faith a "new and everlasting covenant" and rejected the validity and effectiveness of water baptisms conducted by all Christian churches.[5] From its very origins, Mormonism was established by Smith as completely exclusive of all Christian churches.

The First Few Months of Mormonism

Joseph Smith's first few months of functioning as God's last-day prophet produced increasing internal tensions and external opposition. Yet Smith is said to have received direct encouraging words from God that enabled him to endure and press forward. It is claimed that God confirmed that he would curse anyone who did not support Smith and called him to continue to write what was supernaturally shown him.[6]

The thirty or so New York Mormons who were spread throughout Manchester, Fayette, and Colesville Townships[7] gathered on June 9, 1830, for the first church conference at the farmhouse of Peter Whitmer, where Smith provided enthusiastic exhortations to keep the faith. He then returned to Pennsylvania.

Throughout the summer months of 1830, Joseph Smith immediately began working on his own inspired revision of the Bible—today's *Joseph Smith Translation*—claiming that he was able to receive biblical information and interpretations unknown to any Christian since the time of Jesus Christ.[8] This historical fact reveals a deep mistrust of the content of the Bible from the earliest days of Mormonism's existence.

In June 1830 Smith also received a startling revelation of Moses, which is today recorded in the first chapter of the book of Moses. Its content has no Old Testament familiarity to Christians. It is a grand vision of creation and describes Moses as a Christian. In fact, Smith's book of Moses entirely Christianizes the Old Testament and speaks about multiple earths and heavens in order to bring humans to eternal life. Soon following the Moses revelation, Smith also began redoing the early chapters of Genesis, including a major extrabiblical elaboration concerning Enoch.[9]

The Mormons in New York (1830–1831)

In late August 1830, still being strongly opposed by Emma's father, Isaac Hale, Joseph and Emma Smith decided to move from Pennsylvania to Fayette, New York, where they began living with the David Whittier family.

In September 1830, only a few weeks after moving to Fayette, Smith was required to reestablish his sole claim as the Mormon Prophet and authoritative holder of the keys of the kingdom of God when Mormon Hiram Page began declaring that he also was receiving revelations through the aid of a seer stone. Several Mormons followed Page, including Smith's personal scribe, Oliver Cowdery. From the origins of Mormonism Smith had claimed that God compared him to biblical Moses and announced that he alone was the leader of the Mormon Church.[10]

The Location of America's Zion

As early as the summer of 1828, the Lamanites—American Indians—were included in Smith's revelations,[11] and now another Smith revelation unveiled the exact location of the city of Zion as being "on the borders by the Lamanites." *Doctrine and Covenants* 28:9 reads:

> And now, behold, I say unto you that it is not revealed, and no man knoweth where the city Zion shall be built, but it shall be given hereafter. Behold, I say unto you that it shall be on the borders by the Lamanites.

Smith's prophetic declaration that the city of Zion was located on the border of the western Indian territory of the American continent drove the Mormons westward toward Missouri. The Saints believed that the American Indians were the ancestors of the *Book of Mormon* Lamanite people, and the actual offspring of Israel.[12] There were great salvation promises for the Lamanites, and the Mormons were eager to evangelize them.[13]

Mormon Missionaries Sent to the American Indians

Through Joseph Smith revelations, God commissioned Oliver Cowdery, Peter Whitmer, Ziba Peterson, and Parley Pratt to go and evangelize the Lamanites in the far west.[14] On October 18, 1830, only a few weeks following the second church conference, this Mormon mission team departed New York on their fifteen-hundred-mile western trek.

As these missionaries traveled toward Missouri and the Indian borderland, they stopped in Kirtland, Ohio, near Cleveland. Parley Pratt had once lived in Kirtland, where he belonged to the Christian restorationist movement called the *Campbellites*—founded by Alexander Campbell and a local church led by the enthusiastic preacher Sidney Rigdon. Through their witness, Rigdon converted to Mormonism and transferred his entire hundred-member congregation into the Mormon Church. The assimilation of Rigdon's Campbellite church members is extremely important in understanding the initial growth of Mormonism.

Rejoicing, the Mormon mission team traveled west several more weeks and finally reached Independence, Missouri, on January 13, 1831.[15] Although evangelizing the American Indian did not produce significant results in the end, the Mormon growth in Ohio was significant. In fact, within months there were more Mormons in Ohio than in New York.

Joseph Smith's New Bible Scribe

In December 1830, converted Campbellite pastor Sidney Rigdon traveled from Ohio to New York to meet and converse with Joseph Smith concerning the things of God and Mormonism.[16] At the time of Rigdon's visit, Joseph Smith was enthusiastically writing his revision of the Bible. While he was meeting with Rigdon, Smith received a revelation declaring Rigdon another John the Baptist and commissioned him to be his new Bible scribe.[17]

Joseph Smith's Revelation to Move to Ohio

Immediately following Sidney Rigdon's December visit, Joseph Smith—after living in New York for less than six months and only eight months after starting the first Mormon church—had a revolutionary prophetic revelation that would change Mormonism forever. He declared that it was God's will to move the Mormon headquarters from New York to Ohio.[18] At this time, God reportedly told Smith to delay his revision work on the Bible until he arrived in Ohio.[19]

By gathering in Ohio, they would leave all the "Mormon-haters" behind in New York and take one large step closer to the city of Zion near the Indian borderland of Missouri.[20] Following the third church conference on January 2, 1831, Mormons immediately began to sell their homes and property to follow Smith three hundred miles to Kirtland, Ohio, in the dead of winter.

The Mormons in Ohio (1831–1838)

Joseph and Emma Smith, Sidney Rigdon, and Edward Partridge departed New York for Ohio at the end of January 1831, arriving at Newel Whitney's Kirtland store in early February.[21] Smith introduced himself to the Whitneys with the phrase, "I am Joseph Smith the Prophet." Kirtland, Ohio, had been settled for only about twenty years, and had only a few thousand residents. The Smiths initially lived at the Whitney store, which became the new Mormon Church headquarters. It was in this store that Smith received many new revelations.[22]

Ohio's Challenging Early Months

For the first seven months or so—from early February 1831 to late August 1831—Joseph Smith and the other Mormons in Ohio were faced with significant practical and spiritual challenges.

By the middle of May, most of the New York Mormons had sold their possessions and migrated to Kirtland and the surrounding areas. With the rapid Mormon growth in Ohio, and because many New York Mormons had sold everything they owned, Joseph Smith faced many logistical and economic difficulties. In these early months in Ohio, Smith had to put a lot of energy into providing stability, putting his Mormon society in order, and establishing his sole rule over his church.[23]

Many of the early converts to Mormonism in Kirtland were members of a Christian society known as "Disciples." The Disciples were steeped in the practice of communal living and shared all their property. Even after converting to Mormonism, they continued their practice of property-sharing.[24] On February 4, 1831, Smith received the "Law of Consecration" revelation.[25] This revelation built on the Disciples' influence and promoted a plan of economic redistribution among the Mormons. Using Bible passages such as Acts 2:44–45, Smith implemented an economic program and cooperative venture to meet the growing economic demands of the Mormon Church. Mormons were required to deed all their property to the Mormon bishop, who would distribute land to those in need.[26]

But the Mormon redistribution of property simply did not work very well. Later the Law of Consecration was modified to allow private ownership, and Mormons were required only to give their surplus property to the LDS Church. The 1838 Law of Tithing began to take preeminence over the Law of Consecration in Mormonism, although the Law of Consecration revelation has inspired Mormon volunteerism and common support among its members.[27]

In these early Ohio years, Smith also had to address significant spiritual problems.[28] Smith reported that many "strange notions and false spirits" were active among the Ohio people, for many of them were declaring visions and revelations they had received. Once again, Smith had to reestablish himself as the sole revelator and Prophet of the Mormon Church—something that repeatedly occurred throughout his lifetime.[29]

Zion Is in Missouri

The summer of 1831 marked a major development in Mormonism. During the June LDS Church conference, Joseph Smith led the Mormons in a deep pursuit for an endowment of spiritual power that would descend on the gathered Latter-day Saints. This conference saw spiritual endowment and ordained priesthood authority united within Mormonism. Before 1831, men had been called to function in church offices, but they were not ordained to the Melchizedek Priesthood. From this time forward, the powers of the Melchizedek Priesthood would grow to become one of the exclusive teachings of Mormonism. Eventually, a person's quest for being endowed with spiritual power would be experienced in the temple through the exercise of priesthood authority.[30]

Shortly after the fourth Mormon conference on June 3, 1831,[31] Joseph Smith received a revelation commissioning some of the Mormons to further migrate to the western border of Missouri, where they would inherit Zion and the New Jerusalem.[32] Mormon missionaries were sent out two by two, preaching their way to Missouri. Joseph Smith and others departed Kirtland on June 19 for the nine-hundred-mile journey.[33]

Although the Mormons knew Zion was somewhere in Missouri,[34] they were not sure of the exact location. On arriving in Jackson County, Missouri, however, Joseph Smith received a prophetic revelation on July 20 declaring that Independence, Missouri, was America's Promised Land and the city of Zion.[35]

Hearken, O ye elders of my church, saith the Lord your God, who have assembled yourselves together, according to my commandments, in this land, which is the land of Missouri, which is the land which I have appointed and consecrated for the gathering of the saints. Wherefore, this is the land of promise, and the place for the city of Zion. And thus saith the Lord your God, if you will receive wisdom here is wisdom. Behold, the place which is now called Independence is the center place; and a spot for the temple is lying westward, upon a lot which is not far from the courthouse.[36]

Not only was today's Kansas City suburb of Independence the Mormon Zion, but Joseph Smith also declared that it had once been the approximate location of the biblical garden of Eden,[37] and was the spot where Christ's second coming and millennial reign would one day take place.

Through revelation, Joseph Smith called the Saints to purchase as much cheap Missouri land as possible.[38] With great expectation and eschatological ceremony, Smith presided over the celebrative dedication of the new holy city and temple site of Zion on August 2, 1831.[39] It is important to understand that early Mormons were not simply interested in building churches and temples within cities; their vision was to become a church that consisted of a large network of Mormon cities, with the city of Zion as their capital. Mormons wanted whole cities, not simply a portion of them. It is no surprise that the Mormon vision of building and dominating cities created significant tension wherever they settled among non-Mormon citizens.[40]

In obedience to a previous revelation,[41] the Saints held the first Missouri church conference on August 4, and then began their long journey back to Ohio only a few days later. Smith also envisioned Independence as a Mormon publishing center and oversaw the start of the first LDS newspaper, called the *Evening and Morning Star.*

Ohio's Pre-Temple Years (1831–1836)

After spending approximately one month in Independence, Missouri—the New Jerusalem—Joseph Smith and his traveling companions returned to Ohio in late August 1831.[42] Smith—

now approximately twenty-five years old—gave a glowing, detailed report to the Ohio Saints concerning the newly discovered land of Zion, and immediately moved to Hiram, Ohio, located approximately thirty miles south of Kirtland, where he began to work again on his new Bible revision and organize his revelations for publication.[43]

The next four and a half years before the Kirtland temple was built—from late August 1831 to March 27, 1836—was a time of new doctrines, new revelations, and the beginning of the practice of polygamy.

Although Joseph Smith had begun his inspired revision of the Bible back in New York during the summer of 1830, it was during his first few years in Ohio that he zealously dedicated much of his time to it. Numerous Ohio revelations recorded in the *Doctrine and Covenants* are the direct result of Smith's revision of the Bible.[44]

Throughout his life, Joseph Smith emphasized that many salvation truths were missing from the Bible, and that he was the chosen instrument of God to edit and add to its pages.[45] Although Smith announced on July 2, 1833, that his Bible revision was completed, it would never be published in its entirety. Yet the influence of Joseph Smith's revision of the Bible was extremely significant in creating and shaping many of the official Mormon doctrines and practices used today.[46]

During this time, along with the revelatory establishment of the Quorum of the Twelve Apostles and the Quorum of the Seventy,[47] Joseph Smith received and recorded some of today's most controversial revelations, such as the Mormon belief in three heavenly kingdoms,[48] the preexistence of humans, and the LDS priesthood.[49]

In addition, since 1831, Joseph Smith had kept private his personal belief in polygamy. In 1833, however, he married his second wife, Fanny Alger, putting his faith into practice. From 1833 on, Mormonism's exclusivity from Christianity would harden through the practice of polygamy, especially by Mormon Church leaders.

The Doctrine and Covenants

Approximately three months following the organization of the first Mormon church in April 1830, Joseph Smith had already begun copying and arranging the revelations that he claimed to be receiving directly from God. Smith would often provide written copies of these revelations to leaders and missionaries. Now that William Phelps had opened a Mormon printing shop in Missouri, however, he desired to have his revelations printed and bound in book form.

On November 20, 1831, the Mormon leadership sent Oliver Cowdery and John Whitmer to Missouri with Smith's revelations, in order to have Phelps print three thousand copies of what was then called the *Book of Commandments*.[50] The *Book of Commandments* consisted of 160 pages of Smith's revelations. After a major revision, these revelations were republished as the *Book of Doctrine and Covenants* on August 17, 1835.

Smith's Book of Abraham

An Italian explorer discovered several mummies and papyrus scrolls on the west bank of the Nile River near the ancient Egyptian city of Thebes. During their exhibition throughout the United States, these mummies and papyri were displayed in Kirtland, Ohio, in June 1835.[51]

What is crucial in understanding the origin of Mormon Scriptures is the historical fact that Joseph Smith bought several of these papyri, and declared through revelation that they contained the ancient lost writings of biblical Abraham and Joseph. By the same so-called revelatory spirit and power of divine translation through which he had produced the *Book of Mormon*, Smith also claimed to have translated these papyri into what is known today as the book of Abraham. The book of

Abraham has been officially included in the Mormon scriptural collection of the *Pearl of Great Price*. Chapter 5 will cover more details concerning the surprising discovery of these original papyri, and how Joseph Smith's book of Abraham translation actually turned out to be anything but a direct translation as initially claimed.

Ohio's Temple and Apostasy Years (1836–1838)

The two years following the completion of the Kirtland temple—from March 1836 to early 1838—were the highest and lowest times for the Ohio Mormons.

The Mormons in Ohio labored for three years, from 1833 to 1836, building the first LDS temple, which cost approximately $50,000. On March 27, 1836—approximately six years after the organization of the first Mormon church in New York—the seven-hour dedication of the first Mormon temple was apparently filled with many supernatural signs and wonders,[52] including speaking in tongues, prophesying, visions, seeing heavenly visitors such as the apostle Peter, and angelic choirs.[53] It was the Mormon day of Pentecost:

> A noise was heard like the sound of a rushing mighty wind which filled the temple and all the congregation simultaneously arose, being moved upon by an invisible power; many began to speak in tongues and prophesy; others saw glorious visions; and I beheld the temple filled with angels.[54]

As we have seen, early Mormonism was founded on the reports of heavenly visitations, such as Father God, Jesus, Moroni, John the Baptist, and the apostles Peter, James, and John. Again on April 3, 1836, a week after the official dedication of the temple, Smith recorded that Jesus Christ, Moses, and Elijah had also visited him and Oliver Cowdery in the Kirtland temple to reaffirm their exclusive priesthood authority to administer the keys of the kingdom of God on earth.[55] The appearance of Elijah is very significant to the Mormons in that it represented for them the fulfillment of receiving the promised keys of Elijah recorded in *Doctrine and Covenants* 2. It was during this special Elijah visitation that the authority to seal, bind, and loose was conferred on the Mormon leaders. The Elijah keys to bind and loose on earth and heaven relate directly to Latter-day Saints' perceived ability to provide salvation to the dead.

Following the first temple dedication, the Mormons faced major financial problems. In a state of desperation, Joseph Smith took a long trip to Salem, Massachusetts, on another treasure hunt in July 1836. Smith hoped to find treasure—a common pattern during his life—that was apparently hidden under a Salem house.[56] In the end, no treasure was discovered, and he returned to Kirtland empty-handed. This is how the official LDS *Doctrine and Covenants Student Manual* explains Smith's Salem treasure hunt:

> There came to Kirtland a brother by the name of Burgess who stated that he had knowledge of a large amount of money secreted in the cellar of a certain house in Salem, Massachusetts, which had belonged to a widow then deceased, and thought he was the only person who had knowledge of it, or of the location in the house. The brethren accepting representations of Burgess as true made the journey to Salem to secure, if possible, the treasure. Burgess met the brethren in Salem, but claimed that time had wrought such changes in the town that he could not for a certainty point out the house and soon left.[57]

Needing money badly, Smith decided to start his own private bank on January 2, 1837, which he named the Kirtland Safety Society Anti-Banking Company. The collapse of Smith's private bank led to the downfall of Ohio Mormonism.[58] In March 1838, a warrant was issued for Smith's arrest on bank fraud.

Consequently, late one night, Joseph Smith, Sidney Rigdon, and other church leaders fled to Missouri.

What happened next in Ohio is often identified by Mormons as the "great apostasy." During these dark times of economic trouble and chaos in Ohio, many Mormons simply hit bottom physically and spiritually and made the rational decision to leave the Mormon Church. Between November 1837 and June 1838, several hundred people left Mormonism.[59]

By July 1838, only a few years following the Pentecost dedication of the Kirtland temple, the Mormons who remained faithful to Joseph Smith totally abandoned Ohio for Missouri, the Mormons' holy land of Zion. By early 1838, the past Mormon glory of Kirtland, along with its temple, had all but disappeared.

It is interesting to note that between the dedication of the Kirtland temple on March 27, 1836, until Joseph Smith fled Kirtland in early 1838, only two brief Smith revelations were recorded. In fact, from the flight from Kirtland to his death on June 27, 1844, only approximately twenty new revelations were added to Mormonism's *Doctrine and Covenants*.[60]

The Mormons in Missouri (1831–1838)

Mormons had been gathering and settling in Missouri territory since the summer of 1831. Initially—for approximately two years—the gathering of the Saints in Smith's land of Zion was rather peaceful. But Mormons kept flooding into Independence, and the original non-Mormon settlers of the region became very concerned about being outnumbered and overtaken. The tensions between the Mormons and the state of Missouri continued to heat up, eventually disintegrating into mob violence.

On July 20, 1833, many of the non-Mormon settlers entered Independence and demanded that the Mormons leave immediately. When the Mormons refused, a violent mob went on a rampage, destroying the Mormon printing press, stores, and houses. The Mormons were eventually expelled from Jackson County, and they fled across the Missouri River into Clay County, where they set up temporary residences.[61]

Aware of the ongoing tribulations of the Missouri Mormons, Joseph Smith—now only twenty-eight years old and still living in Ohio—decided in February 1834 to organize a Mormon Army of God called *Zion's Camp* and to go and defend the Saints in Missouri from the violent "Mormon-haters." Although full of good intentions, Zion's Camp would never be able to fight hundreds of armed Missouri settlers. The Mormon army faced insurmountable odds. Soon Joseph Smith received a revelation[62] in which he announced that the redemption day of Zion had not yet arrived. He dismantled Zion's army and sent his Mormon soldiers back to Ohio.

As a result of Smith's dismantling of his army, the disillusionment among the Mormons grew. Many disgusted Mormons left Smith, but those who remained faithful—such as Brigham Young—were rewarded and promoted into the top echelons of Mormon Church leadership.

Taking Refuge in Northern Missouri

As the situation was getting worse in Independence, Missouri, Mormons began fleeing into Clay County, where they started a new Mormon city at Far West. It was in Far West that Joseph Smith and the Mormon leadership would eventually make their headquarters in March 1838 after abandoning Ohio. And it was here in Far West that the secret military group called the *Danites* was organized to defend the Mormons.

Attempting to get a new start, reestablish authority, and obtain badly needed finances, Joseph Smith changed the name of the Mormon Church to The Church of Jesus Christ of Latter-day Saints on April 26, 1838,[63] attributing the fulfillment of the prophecy of Isaiah 11:1–10 to himself instead of Jesus Christ.[64] Smith presented and implemented his vision of the Law of Tithing at Far West as well.[65]

As opposition to the Mormons continued to increase in Clay County, the Missouri legislature decided to create Caldwell County, where the Mormons could live in isolation from non-Mormons. From Caldwell, Joseph Smith began searching for other locations in northern Missouri where emigrating Saints could create new settlements.

In May 1838, Joseph Smith made one of the most astonishing declarations he had ever made. While visiting Daviess County, seventy miles to the north of the city of Independence, Smith claimed to have discovered the literal spot where Adam had settled after God expelled him and Eve from the garden of Eden, and where Adam would return before the second coming of Christ.[66] Smith apparently pointed out the exact spot where he said Adam had once had his altar. The Mormons called this newly dedicated settlement *Adam-ondi-Ahman*,[67] which apparently means "the place or land of God where Adam dwelt" in the pure Adamic language, according to Smith.[68] Mormon apostle Bruce McConkie describes this LDS teaching:

> At that great gathering Adam offered sacrifices on an altar built for the purpose. A remnant of that very altar remained on the spot down through the ages. On May 19, 1838 Joseph Smith and a number of his associates stood on the remainder of the pile of stones at a place called Spring Hill, Daviess County, Missouri. There the Prophet taught them that Adam again would visit in the Valley of Adam-ondi-Ahman, holding a great council as a prelude to the great and dreadful day of the Lord.[69]

During the summer months of 1838, northern Missouri was getting dangerous as a "Mormon War" was feared. The locals believed that the Mormons were preparing to conquer all of Missouri, and they wanted them to leave their state. When

Joseph Smith and other Mormon leaders were jailed at the end of 1838,[70] the Mormons fled Missouri into Illinois and Iowa under the leadership of Brigham Young.

The Mormons in Illinois (1839–1846)

By the thousands, desperate Mormons fled east across the Mississippi River into the area of Quincy, Illinois—approximately two hundred miles from Far West—where they settled temporarily. After Joseph Smith—now thirty-three years old—was released from jail in April 1839, he immediately joined his Mormon flock in Illinois.

Under Smith's leadership, the Mormons looked once again for a permanent gathering place. They purchased land on the Mississippi River and began to build their new Mormon city they called *Nauvoo*—meaning "city beautiful"—where the Latter-day Saints would live out their faith for approximately the next five years until the death of their Prophet, Joseph Smith.

The Problems of Theocracy and Polygamy

The Mormons lived peacefully in Nauvoo from 1839 to 1842, but then major trouble began. The primary problems were rooted in the fact that the Mormons ran Nauvoo as a powerful church-theocracy with their own militia, and also practiced polygamy. Theocracy and polygamy in Illinois were simply not acceptable to the local non-Mormon population.

Joseph Smith's Controversial Revelations and Sermon

During Joseph Smith's last few years in the city of Nauvoo before his death in 1844, many of his most unusual and controversial revelations, teachings, and rituals were introduced and developed in the LDS Church. Along with Smith's becoming a Master Mason in March 1842,[71] he revealed his doctrines of water baptism for the dead,[72] a special endowment ritual, God's having a body of flesh and bones,[73] and eternal marriage and polygamy.[74]

Many Latter-day Saints consider Joseph Smith's outdoor sermon at the funeral of Mormon Elder King Follett on April 7, 1844, in Nauvoo, Illinois, to be one of his greatest.[75] This sermon was part of the general church conference, and it was also one of the last sermons Smith preached. He died less than three months after delivering it. Joseph Smith's "King Follett Discourse" was certainly one of his most revealing and troubling sermons from a doctrinal perspective.

Smith's King Follett sermon unveiled his beliefs that God had once been a man, that a human could become a god, that matter is eternal, and that many gods together had organized—not created—the world out of chaotic matter. The content of Smith's Follett sermon has long been recognized, quoted, and affirmed as containing official Mormon doctrine. By the Nauvoo years, it had become clear that the teaching and practices of Joseph Smith's LDS Church resembled none of the major branches of Christianity.

Joseph Smith Runs for President

Joseph Smith decided to run for the presidency of the United States in January 1844, at which time he rejected America's political parties and founded the Council of Fifty to direct his presidential campaign. Smith desired to establish God's political kingdom over non-Mormons in preparation for the second coming of Christ.[76] He sent out Mormon missionaries across the nation to promote his presidential candidacy. But Smith's grand political scheme collapsed when he was arrested with other Mormon leaders for treason and jailed in the city of Carthage, Missouri.

The Death of Joseph Smith

While Joseph Smith and other Mormon leaders were await-ing trial in the Carthage jail, a group of men entered and shot Joseph and his brother Hyrum to death. June 27, 1844, is recognized by the LDS Church as the day in which their Prophet was martyred at the young age of thirty-eight.[77] The next day, on June 28, Joseph Smith's body was returned to Nauvoo, where thousands of Mormons were in shock that their founder and Prophet was dead. What would they do now?

three

FROM JOSEPH SMITH
TO SALT LAKE CITY

Joseph Smith's death led to a bitter succession crisis not unlike what had occurred following the death of Muhammad. Since Smith had not officially named his successor, his death caused great confusion and deep spiritual hopelessness among his followers in the Mormon city of Nauvoo. Many questions needed to be answered, but the most important one was who would succeed Joseph Smith as the ultimate Prophet of Mormonism.

The Succession Crisis and Brigham Young (1844–1846)

Initially, the succession process to replace Joseph Smith seemed like a chaotic free-for-all. At the time of Smith's murder, the majority of the LDS Twelve Apostles were in the eastern United States, preaching and campaigning for Smith's presidency. Once they received the bad news of Smith's death, they rushed back to Nauvoo. But Sidney Rigdon, once Smith's primary Bible scribe and a longtime Mormon leader, had already arrived in Nauvoo from Pittsburgh, claiming that he should be the future guardian of the church.

A few days later, just in time, Brigham Young, the president of the Quorum of the Twelve Apostles, and many of the other apostles arrived to oppose Rigdon, whom they considered to be a Mormon apostate.

A special church conference was called on August 8, 1844, in order to make the final decision on Smith's replacement. Rigdon spoke first, arguing that he was the chosen of God. When Brigham Young spoke, however, it was reported that he seemed to be transfigured into Joseph Smith himself; it was claimed that even his voice sounded like Smith's. Many interpreted the transfiguration of Young as proof that God's prophetic mantle had fallen on him.[1] Through an almost unanimous vote by the conference members, the decision was made to replace Joseph Smith with Brigham Young, and Sidney Rigdon was officially excommunicated from the LDS Church.

Immediately following the appointment of the new Mormon successor, there was a major split between Brigham Young and Joseph Smith's wife Emma. In fact, it seems rather revealing that Young never even visited Emma after Joseph's death. Emma disapproved of Young and was emphatic that her husband had ordained their eleven-year-old son, Joseph III, as his successor. In the end, however, she was ignored and shunned. When the Mormons departed for the Salt Lake Valley, Emma Smith refused to go, and she remained in Nauvoo, Illinois, and eventually remarried.

In 1860, the Reorganized Church of Jesus Christ of Latter Day Saints—now the Community of Christ[2]—would be started in Independence, Missouri, with Joseph Smith III becoming its first president. Today, it owns Joseph Smith's grave and his two homes in Nauvoo, Illinois.

The Mormon Migration to Utah (1846–1847)

During the year following Joseph Smith's death, Brigham Young and the LDS Twelve Apostles began to focus their attention on the Great Salt Lake Valley west of the Rocky Mountains as the new destination for the Mormon Zion. At this time, the Utah Territory was a poorly defined and loosely governed Mexican province. Young and the other LDS apostles desired a new Mormon gathering place that was in total isolation from the non-Mormon world. They concluded that the desolate Salt Lake Valley was just the place to build their Mormon version of the kingdom of God on earth.

The Six-Month Trek to Utah

The Mormons were planning to leave Illinois in the spring of 1846. But they feared that federal military troops were coming to attack Nauvoo; and so it was that in February, Mormon wagons hurried across the frozen Mississippi River into Iowa, tearfully looking back at what they called the *City of Joseph*. They waited out the brutally cold winter, and that spring the Saints began the two-thousand-mile trek to Utah. The Mormons marched for five months across the three hundred miles of Iowa plains; and by summer they had reached the valley of the Missouri River, which was the western Iowa border.[3]

Hundreds of Mormons gathered at a location called Winter Quarters, near Omaha, Nebraska. The strategic plan was that the majority of Mormons would settle at Winter Quarters through the winter of 1846–1847 while a pioneer group led by Brigham Young pushed on into the Salt Lake Valley to establish an encampment and begin planting crops. The vanguard group led by Brigham Young reached the Salt Lake Valley on July 24, 1847.[4]

The Mormons in Utah

Brigham Young named the Salt Lake region *Deseret*, which is a word from the *Book of Mormon* meaning "beehive."[5] This was symbolic of Young's vision that the new Zion would become a hive of cooperative activity and prosperity, a totally independent Mormon society operating only under Joseph Smith's revelatory laws of God.

While the early pioneers worked hard to prepare for the hundreds of Mormons who would arrive in the valley, Brigham Young returned to Winter Quarters to help lead the waiting Mormons to the new Zion. It was in Winter Quarters that Young was officially ordained the second President and Prophet of the Latter-day Saints on December 5, 1847, three years after the death of Joseph Smith.

The first company[6] of wagons led by Brigham Young left Winter Quarters on April 16, 1847, on the thousand-mile journey across the Rocky Mountains to Utah. Located on the north side of the Platte River, the Mormon Trail paralleled the Oregon Trail. In 1847, thirteen separate companies of Mormon pioneers totaling approximately two thousand made the Utah journey. Although the first trek has become celebrated, the migration of Mormons to the Utah Territory continued for more than ten years.

Utah Mormonism under Brigham Young (1847–1877)

The word *isolated* best describes Utah Mormonism under the thirty-year rule of Brigham Young from 1847 to 1877, the longest reigning Prophet the Mormons have ever had. When the Mormons first arrived in Utah's Great Salt Lake Basin, they were very happy in their self-imposed segregation from their Gentile enemies. They could now build their version of the kingdom of God in peace and self-sufficiency.

As we will see in this chapter, however, the early exclusive Mormonism created by Joseph Smith and Brigham Young would be required to go through many significant developments and changes over the next half-century, from July 24, 1846, to January 4, 1896. These many changes would be required before the Great Salt Lake Valley would be considered politically and legally worthy by the United States government to become an official American state.

Mormons in Mexican Territory (1847–1850)

For the first three years following their arrival in the Great Salt Lake Valley, the Mormons lived in Mexican land outside of the jurisdiction and laws of the United States. As a result, the Mormons were totally free to live under the practical organizing skill of Brigham Young and operate openly as an LDS Church theocracy.[7]

The first major task was to determine the place to build a new Mormon city. Within the first few days of their Salt Lake arrival, Young chose ten acres on which to build a temple. Today, it is known as Temple Square in Salt Lake City.

Salt Lake City was designed around Temple Square. The Mormon leaders of the First Presidency and the Quorum of Twelve Apostles were given plots of land near the temple site where they could build their homes. Brigham Young built a long row of log houses where his wives and families could live. Every street of the city was numbered running parallel to the four sides of the temple site. The city streets were divided up into wards, and each ward was overseen by a Mormon bishop.

During the first few years, the Mormons struggled to survive. Although they worked extremely hard, it was the California gold rush that provided the supplies and finances that they needed to turn the desert into Zion.[8] In 1849, thousands of non-Mormons traveled through the Salt Lake Valley to California, and they were willing to buy goods from the Mormons at inflated prices. Although Brigham Young hated the interaction with the non-Mormon Gentiles, the gold-rush income served to provide the Mormons with the finances they needed. By the 1850s, many new Mormon towns were being established, colleges being started, and hundreds of Saints being settled that were supported by gold-rush money.

Mormons in American Territory (1850–1896)

With the end of the Mexican War, the United States gained possession of the Salt Lake Valley in 1848. It was officially declared an American territory in 1850. Although the Mormons wanted the territory to be officially named *Deseret*, Congress decided instead to name it *Utah*, after the Ute Indians who lived in the region.

The Mormons lived for approximately forty-six years—from 1850 to 1896—within America's Utah Territory. Initially, Brigham Young was appointed Utah's territorial governor. He took his oath of office on February 3, 1851. With American recognition, Young moved aggressively and strategically to build the Mormon version of the kingdom of God in the Utah Territory. Young was pragmatic, strong-willed, and determined, even if it meant standing against the laws of the United States.

When non-Mormon judges and appointed officials arrived in the Utah Territory in 1851, they were shocked to discover a Mormon theocracy and the practice of polygamy. When they returned east, they provided a detailed report to President Millard Fillmore, which created an ongoing suspicion in Washington, D.C., concerning Mormon Utah.

In 1852, Brigham Young—who had many wives—announced boldly that polygamy was now an authorized practice of the LDS Church. In 1854, Young also built a large, beautiful home that became known as his Beehive House because of the roof's beehive-shaped cupola. It was from the Beehive House that Young served as both governor and Prophet, and a connecting structure housed his many wives and children.

Starting in 1854, the Republican Party's platform denounced the twin evils of slavery and polygamy. When Republican James Buchanan became U.S. President in 1857, he replaced Brigham Young as territorial governor of Utah with non-Mormon Alfred Cumming and sent an army to Utah to enforce the change. As a result, what has become known as the Utah War began. In defiance of federal troops, Young called the Mormons to prepare to defend themselves. They created blockades and dug trenches in preparation for a battle. Young had instructed the Mormons to burn everything, rather than surrender to federal forces. In the end, things settled down, and Governor Cumming was finally accepted by the Mormons, albeit reluctantly. But it was also during this time of LDS distrust of and resistance toward outsiders that on September 11, 1857, Mormons attacked an unarmed non-Mormon wagon train, killing more than a hundred innocent people.[9] This dark episode in Mormon history is called the *Mountain Meadows Massacre*.

Although the Civil War distracted much of the nation from the practices of the Mormons, in 1862 Abraham Lincoln did sign into law the Morrill Anti-Bigamy Act, which made polygamy in America a crime and limited the amount of property that the LDS Church could own. Until the Civil War was over in 1865, there was little enforcement of the Morrill Act, and the Mormons continued to build the Salt Lake temple, start public-works projects, and build more settlements.

Mormon isolationism, however, was greatly threatened when in 1869 America's transcontinental railroad made traveling to Utah no longer a major undertaking. Brigham Young's last years were invested in promoting Mormon cooperative businesses as he saw his isolationist form of Mormonism facing great dangers from non-Mormon settlers and the potential enforcement of America's anti-polygamy laws.

Brigham Young died on August 29, 1877, at the age of seventy-six. He had married at least twenty wives and fathered fifty-six children.[10] Through his self-determination, the Mormon population eventually grew in the Utah Territory to approximately 135,000.[11] After Brigham Young's death, Utah Mormonism would be required to make significant changes before receiving acceptance and legitimacy in America.

Utah Mormonism after Brigham Young (1877–1896)

The next two decades following the death of Brigham Young—from 1877 to 1896—were characterized by an outright battle between Mormonism and the United States over the issues of LDS theocracy and polygamy.

Following the death of Brigham Young, John Taylor became the third Mormon President and Prophet in October 1880, the same year that the fiftieth anniversary of the Mormon Church was celebrated. Taylor's revelation promoting the LDS practice of polygamy in 1886 set the stage for a major showdown with the United States government. He declared:

> I have not revoked this [polygamy] law nor will I for it is ever-lasting and those who will enter into my glory must obey the conditions thereof, even so amen.[12]

Mormons Go Underground

Taylor's declaration was a proclamation of defiance against the
United States' newly passed Edmunds-Tucker Act in 1882,
once again outlawing the practice of polygamy.

Because Mormons refused to follow American anti-polygamy
law, over the next few years hundreds of resistant Mormons
were jailed. Many of the Mormon men practicing polygamy,
including LDS leadership, went underground. On July 25,
1887, Prophet Taylor died on the run from the United States
federal authorities.

The United States simply would not accept a self-proclaimed
independent theocratic kingdom to exist in open defiance
of the laws of the nation. In 1887, the United States passed
a law that dissolved the Mormon Church organization, and
required all property worth over $50,000 to be turned over
to the federal government. In 1890, it was also determined
that Mormons would not be able to vote. The very existence
of the Mormon theocratic society was in danger of collapsing,
and a revelation from God was the only answer.

The 1890 Manifesto and Utah Statehood

On April 7, 1889, the fourth President and Prophet, Wilford
Woodruff, began leading the LDS Church. Woodruff reported
receiving a revelation from God in September 1890 that authorized him to stop the LDS practice of polygamy. Woodruff's
official declaration against polygamy has come to be known as
the Manifesto, recorded today as Official Declaration 1 located
at the end of the *Doctrine and Covenants*. A second manifesto
would also be made by President and Prophet Joseph F. Smith
in 1904, and a church policy was enacted that would excom-
municate all polygamists.

Following the 1890 Manifesto, the isolated Utah Mormonism shaped under Brigham Young was moving toward accom-
modation and legitimacy. In 1891, they dismantled the Mor-

mon People's Party and began to align themselves with the Republican and Democratic political parties. As a result, church property was soon returned and Utah statehood was near.

Utah Mormons under Statehood (1896–Today)

By the time Utah became an official state on January 4, 1896, Mormons were desiring to assimilate into the mainstream of American life and begin improving their national and public image. Another major step toward American assimilation took place when LDS Prophet Spencer Kimball received a revelation in June 1978, declaring that Mormonism would no longer exclude male blacks from its priesthoods. It is recorded as Official Declaration 2 and is located at the end of the *Doctrine and Covenants*.

The modern LDS Church no longer exhibits the extreme isolationism of nineteenth-century Mormonism created under Joseph Smith and Brigham Young. Instead, Mormonism now works hard at promoting through an extensive public-relations campaign their desire to be accepted in American life.

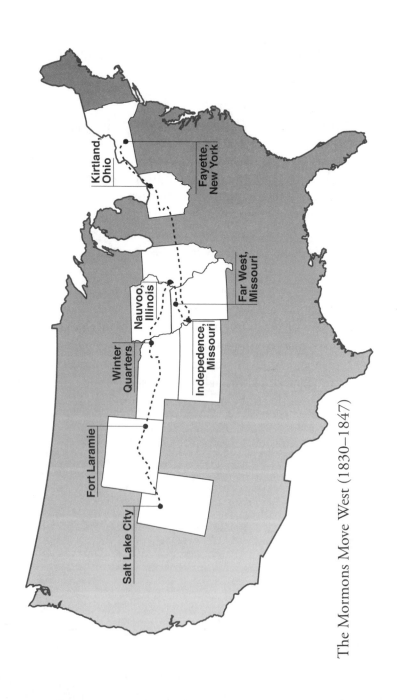

The Mormons Move West (1830–1847)

What Mormonism
Teaches and Why

four

THE ONE AND ONLY TRUE CHURCH ON EARTH

Mormonism declares that it is the only God-authorized, authentically apostolic, revelation-receiving, keys-of-the-kingdom church on the face of the earth today. The LDS Church's central message is that it is the single organized expression of the true New Testament church and the only earthly vehicle of the restored gospel of Jesus Christ in all its fullness. This is how the official Web site of the LDS Church defines the restoration of the gospel (notice its emphasis on being the true church of Jesus Christ on earth today):

> When Jesus Christ was on the earth, He established His Church among His followers. After His Crucifixion and the deaths of His Apostles, the fulness of the gospel was taken from the earth because of widespread apostasy. Through the Prophet Joseph Smith, our Father in Heaven and His Son Jesus Christ restored the fulness of the gospel. The true Church of Jesus Christ is on the earth again. Because of the Restoration, the

teachings and ordinances necessary for salvation are available to all people.[1]

Mormons claim that the LDS Church is the kingdom of God on earth.[2] All Christian churches are excluded. The foundational LDS passage for this exclusive and elite teaching is found in their scriptural book *Doctrine and Covenants* 1:30:

> And also those to whom these commandments were given, might have power to lay the foundation of this church, and to bring it forth out of obscurity and out of darkness, the only true and living church upon the face of the whole earth. . . .

Mormon systematic theologian Bruce McConkie makes these very revealing assertions in his prominent and best-selling book *Mormon Doctrine*:

> If it had not been for Joseph Smith and the restoration, there would be no salvation. There is no salvation outside the Church of Jesus Christ of Latter-day Saints. . . .
>
> This Church is the only true and living church upon the face of the whole earth, the only organization authorized by the Almighty to preach his gospel and administer the ordinances of salvation, the only Church which has power to save and exalt men in the hereafter.[3]

Since Joseph Smith's First Vision experience in AD 1820,[4] Christian churches have been understood to be an abomination to God, and Mormonism has rejected the divine authority and the historical doctrinal creeds of Christianity. The LDS Church believes that every major branch of global Christianity— Protestant, Roman Catholic, and Eastern Orthodox—is unsound and incomplete in its teaching and practices.[5]

Since the LDS Church continually accuses Christians of wrongly and unjustly excluding it from being Christian[6] and strongly publicizes its dismay and disgust toward Christians who identify it as a major cult, the Mormons' exclusive assertion that they are the earth's only true church is not only bold, but to many Christians also offensive, prideful, and very disingenuous.[7]

And so, we must ask the following question: On what authoritative basis can Mormons make such an exclusive and universal claim that they are the only church that possesses divine authority to act on God's behalf today? The answer is found in this chapter.

The Mormon Doctrine of Christian Apostasy

Mormonism bases its absolute exclusive status on its belief that a complete and universal Christian apostasy—a falling away from God—took place immediately following the death of the New Testament apostles. As a result of this so-called destructive Christian apostasy, Mormons propagate the doctrine that the genuine apostolic New Testament church totally disappeared from the face of God's globe. According to LDS teaching, since the second and third centuries AD, the entire world had floundered in spiritual and salvation darkness until God supernaturally restored the fullness of the gospel back to the earth through the fourteen-year-old Joseph Smith in AD 1820. This would mean that for approximately seventeen hundred years, there was no Christian or church existing on the entire planet that could act with effective salvation authority on behalf of God.

The universal Christian apostasy in early church history is a cornerstone doctrine of the LDS Church. It is a crucial teaching because without it Mormonism would cease to exist. The logic is straightforward. Unless a complete Christian apostasy—a universal rebellious onslaught against God's truth—actually caused the New Testament church to collapse and disappear, then there would be no need for a comprehensive restoration of New Testament Christianity, supposedly represented today by the LDS Church. Consequently, Mormonism would be irrelevant, unsubstantiated, and simply untrue.

Satan's Great and Abominable Church

The *Book of Mormon* teaches that two distinct churches exist in the world today: the true church of the Lamb of God—the LDS Church—and Satan's great apostate and abominable Babylon church of Revelation chapter 17.[8] This is how the *Book of Mormon*'s 1 Nephi 14:10 reads:

> And it came to pass that he said unto me: Look, and behold that great and abominable church, which is the mother of abominations, whose founder is the devil. And he said unto me: Behold there are save two churches only; the one is the church of the Lamb of God, and the other is the church of the devil; wherefore, who so belongeth not to the church of the Lamb of God belongeth to that great church, which is the mother of abominations; and she is the whore of all the earth.

Although not all Mormons would necessarily embrace this definition, Bruce McConkie defines Satan's apostate church this way:

> The church of the devil . . . is every false religion, every supposed system of salvation which does not actually save and exalt man in the highest heaven of the Celestial world. It is every church except the true church, whether parading under a Christian or a pagan banner.[9]

Based on McConkie's definition, since no Christian church—whether Protestant, Roman Catholic, or Eastern Orthodox—advocates a Mormon system of salvation that offers humankind exaltation into godhood in the highest Celestial kingdom, then we can conclude that all Christian churches today can be generally categorized within Satan's apostate church.

The Great Christian Apostasy in the Bible

Mormonism carefully isolates certain Bible passages[10] in its effort to prove that an overwhelming Christian falling away and apostasy against God's truth of salvation was already growing and overcoming the New Testament church before the death of Jesus' authorized apostles.

Yet a careful contextual and chronological examination of these handpicked Bible passages used by Mormons reveals that they simply fall short of interpretative accuracy. The Bible does not teach the Mormon apostasy thesis that God's kingdom truth and authority in the New Testament church was in the process of being significantly lost and overcome. This is simply interpretative exaggeration at its best.

Christians accept the fact that we will always live within the history-long conflict between the kingdom of God and the kingdom of darkness until the second coming of Jesus Christ. So New Testament passages warning against and exhorting us to confront false teaching, false christs, and false apostles and prophets are normative and not extraordinary.

We all know that apostasy and rebellion against God began in the garden of Eden, continued through the Old and New Testaments, and will continue on throughout human history. Christians are not naive about Satan's active work against the kingdom of God within and without the church. Yet we have an unwavering trust that God is in total control of his church and world.

Again, the topic of apostasy and false teaching exists in the Bible, but the interpretative issue that divides Christianity and Mormonism is the depth and extensiveness of apostasy that was actually experienced in the New Testament church. Although apostasy was present, the Bible does not teach that it was widespread during New Testament times, much less that it was overcoming the church's very existence.

Christians have no need to entertain or become apostasy alarmists. Throughout history, even when Christians have been unfaithful, God has always remained faithful to continue to build and renew his church.

Satan's Apostate Church in Early Church History

Mormonism not only teaches that a Christian apostasy movement was overtaking the New Testament church, but also believes that Satan's abominable church[11] grew and developed into a widespread organized Christian apostate movement during the second and third centuries AD. Mormons believe that during early church history, this apostate Christian church gained complete dominance that led to the total disappearance of the true church from the earth.

Although Mormonism does not name a specific church or denomination as Satan's historic great and apostate church in earliest Christianity, Mormons do generally identify and describe it as "Hellenized Christianity."[12] They believe that early Christianity compromised the biblical truth and authority of salvation, and became thoroughly Hellenized by Greek culture and philosophy. The Mormon thesis is that as the Christian church spread into the Gentile world, it revised and accommodated biblical truth to a Greek worldview. As a result, Hebraic or biblical Christianity lost out to Hellenized

Christianity, which radically exchanged New Testament truth for human authority, councils, and creeds.

Mormons claim that the Christian church has lost all apostolic authority to act on behalf of God[13] and no longer possesses the fullness of the New Testament gospel, which they identify as the exclusive doctrines and practices of Mormonism.

In the end, however, after all the speculative and generalized talk, the LDS teaching concerning the great Christian apostasy during early Christianity is nothing more than historical patchwork. There is simply no substantial historical support or documentation to uphold such a conspiracy theory, as Dr. Stephen Robinson, Brigham Young University professor, admits:

> This period might be called the blind spot in Christian history, for it is here that the fewest primary historical sources have been preserved. We have good sources for New Testament Christianity; then the lights go out, so to speak, and we hear the muffled sounds of a great struggle. When the lights come on again a hundred or so years later, we find that someone has rearranged all the furniture and Christianity has become something very different from what it was in the beginning.[14]

Grounded in the truth of Matthew 16:18, "I tell you, you are Peter, and on this rock I will build my church, and the gates of hell shall not prevail against it," Christians today stand strong, trusting in God's absolute faithfulness and sovereignty, knowing that he will build his church on the rock of Jesus Christ, and the gates of hell cannot stand up against it.[15]

What about the Protestant Reformation?

Often, in defense of its apostasy doctrine in early Christianity, Mormonism states that the Protestant Reformers—Martin Luther, John Calvin, and others—used many of the same apostasy Bible passages to prove that the Roman Catholic Church was satanic and corrupt. Some Mormons even claim that the Protestant Reformers actually agreed with their great-apostasy doctrine,[16] as Dr. Stephen Robinson seems to indicate below:

> In terms of the doctrine of apostasy—that is, that at some point in time the historical church was no longer the true Church—most Protestants agree with the Latter-day Saints in principle; they just differ on the dates.[17]

But let's be clear. Although the LDS Church states that the Protestant Reformation generated some correction and restoration to true biblical Christianity, it does not remotely conclude that the Protestant Reformation was sufficient or, for that matter, not apostate itself. According to Robert Millet, Brigham Young University professor of ancient Scripture:

> Because apostolic power was not on the earth, Latter-day Saints believe that alterations in doctrine took place during the Reformation as well, theological shifts away from the teachings of the primitive church in the days of Jesus and the apostles. Such doctrines as predestination, man's inability to come unto Christ on his own, salvation by grace alone (good works not essential to salvation), and *sola scriptura*, the notion of the sufficiency of written scripture—each of which is a vital element within current Christian thinking—do not fully reflect the teachings and doctrine of the first few centuries of the Christian church, it was not sufficient. A complete restoration was needed.[18]

Are All Christian Churches Apostate Today?

Since the LDS Church is unwavering toward its official stance that it is the only true and living church on earth, how do

Mormons view and interact with today's non-LDS churches and devout followers of Jesus Christ?

Over the last few years, many Mormons have attempted to publicly soften and smooth out their communication about Christian churches, something that is not easy to do when their scriptural books use the terms *apostate, abomination,* and *corrupt* to describe Christianity. There is no question, however, that LDS Church officials are pushing a much friendlier and more interactive Mormon approach toward outsiders. Mormons are being exhorted from the highest levels of the LDS Church to be nice and engage in cordial interaction and dialogue with Christians.[19]

Although official teaching of the LDS Church continues to emphasize that Christianity today remains deeply flawed, some Mormons are saying that many Christian churches and individuals are well-meaning and possess some truth. As Dr. Stephen Robinson states:

> Informed Latter-day Saints do not argue that historic Christianity lost all truth or became completely corrupt. The orthodox churches may have lost the "fullness" of the gospel, but they did not lose all of it nor even most of it.[20]

The LDS Church emphasizes that Mormonism and Christianity have many moral values in common and encourages working together on humanitarian and political projects in our communities and world. Mormons also make it clear that they do not believe that Christians will go to hell. For example, almost as a token gesture, Dr. Robinson writes:

> Christians in the generic sense are not automatically excluded from salvation as they will still have the opportunity to accept the Mormon gospel in the postmortal life after they die.[21]

Yet despite all the nice talk and gestures, the LDS Church still believes that it is the only one and true church on the earth, emphasizing that although today's Christian churches were not the cause of the great apostasy, they are certainly the offspring of it. Although often saying it with a smile of kindness, Mormonism continues to claim unapologetically that the LDS Church is the kingdom of God on earth, and that it alone possesses apostolic authority and the fullness of the gospel of salvation.[22]

The Male Mormon Priesthoods

At the center of Mormonism's exclusive teaching and practices is the belief that the kingdom of God and salvation are totally governed through LDS priesthood authority.[23] Here is how the LDS Church defines its priesthood:

The priesthood is the eternal power and authority of God. Through the priesthood God created and governs the heavens and the earth. Through this power He redeems and exalts His children, bringing to pass "the immortality and eternal life of man" (Moses 1:39). God gives priesthood authority to worthy male members of the Church so they can act in His name for the salvation of His children. Priesthood holders can be authorized to preach the gospel, administer the ordinances of salvation, and govern the kingdom of God on the earth.[24]

The elite teaching and practices of Mormonism can never be understood apart from the realization that everything in the LDS Church is founded and authorized by the sealing, binding, and loosing power of its male priesthoods.[25] The ordained male priesthoods' authoritative role in the Church of Jesus Christ of Latter-day Saints cannot be overemphasized. The LDS Church's claim that it is the one and only true church on earth is primarily based on its theology of priesthood authority.

The Mormon Church has two distinct male priesthoods—all women are excluded—called the Aaronic Priesthood and the Melchizedek Priesthood.[26]

Mormonism teaches that God delegates his priesthood authority to worthy male members of the LDS Church so that they can act in his name for the salvation of his spirit-children. According to Mormonism, the priesthood holders are the only authorized ones to preach the gospel, administer the ordinances of salvation, and govern the kingdom of God on the earth.

It is also important to understand that eternal salvation in Mormonism is exclusively mediated through its official male priesthoods. The Latter-day Saints' Aaronic and Melchizedek Priesthoods are believed to be the exclusive agents of the delegated power and authority of God on earth for the salvation of humankind.[27] For without the direct authority of the Mormon male priesthood, the LDS ordinances of eternal salvation cannot be performed or experienced.[28] For Mormons, the door of eternal salvation is opened and made possible only through the so-called authoritative keys possessed by the male priesthood. It is actually a very simple equation: without the ordinances performed by the ordained Mormon priesthoods, eternal salvation in Jesus Christ is not available and cannot be experienced.

Although Christians acknowledge the important leadership functions of New Testament apostles, prophets, evangelists, pastors, and teachers to equip the church for the work of ministry (Eph. 4:11–12), we declare that Jesus Christ is the only eternal Mediator and High Priest of God's spiritual authority and power. As apostolic writings make clear, Jesus is the only Mediator between God and men and the only Mediator of a new covenant (1 Tim. 2:5; Heb. 9:15).

The Aaronic Priesthood for Young Men

The Aaronic Priesthood is called the lesser, Levitical, or preparatory priesthood in the LDS Church.[29] A worthy male Mormon who has experienced water baptism can be ordained into the Aaronic Priesthood beginning at age twelve and is given a very special status within the LDS organization. The Aaronic male priesthood holder enters into a detailed preparation process to eventually earn a leadership position within the Melchizedek Priesthood. This is how the LDS Church defines the Aaronic Priesthood:

> Worthy male members may receive the Aaronic Priesthood beginning at age 12. These young men, typically ages 12–17, receive many opportunities to participate in sacred priesthood ordinances and give service. As they worthily fulfill their duties, they act in the name of the Lord to help others receive the blessings of the gospel.[30]

These young male Mormons participate in numerous services and responsibilities, ranging from blessing and serving the sacrament (communion), assisting in temporal matters, collecting offerings, teaching, baptizing, and even ordaining other boys into the Aaronic Priesthood.

The Melchizedek Priesthood for Adult Men

In early Mormon history, the higher and greater priesthood position in the LDS Church was called the Holy Priesthood after the Order of the Son of God. It was eventually changed to the Melchizedek Priesthood.[31] This priesthood office is named after the high priest Melchizedek, who lived during the time of Abraham.[32] The official LDS Web site defines the Melchizedek Priesthood in this way:

> Through the authority of the Melchizedek Priesthood, Church leaders guide the Church and direct the preaching of the gospel throughout the world. In the ordinances of the Melchizedek Priesthood, "the power of godliness is manifest" (D&C 84:20). This greater priesthood was given to Adam and has been on the

earth whenever the Lord has revealed His gospel. It was taken from the earth during the Great Apostasy, but it was restored in 1829, when the Apostles Peter, James, and John conferred it upon Joseph Smith and Oliver Cowdery.[33]

Mormons believe that the Melchizedek Priesthood was first given to Adam and possesses the power and authority over all the offices in the LDS Church.[34] A Mormon male must become a worthy Melchizedek Priesthood holder to receive eternal exaltation into a god, for it is a requirement before he can receive the temple endowment and be sealed to his wife and family for eternity. Bruce McConkie's statement makes the LDS teaching concerning the Melchizedek Priesthood quite clear:

> Without the Melchizedek Priesthood salvation in the kingdom of God would not be available for men on earth . . . As far as all religious organizations now existing are concerned, the presence or the absence of this priesthood establishes the divinity or falsity of a professing church.[35]

Are Mormons Christians?

Although I considered writing a chapter dedicated to the question of whether Mormons are Christians, I concluded that this was not really necessary. First, Dr. Craig Blomberg has already done a superb job in his chapter "Is Mormonism Christian?" in the book *The New Mormon Challenge*,[36] and second, I believe that this question is best addressed in the context of this chapter, which explains Mormonism's exclusive claim that it is the one and only true church on earth. It is clear that Mormonism has set itself totally apart from all Christian churches, whether Protestant, Roman Catholic, or Eastern Orthodox, and itself affirms that it is not Christian as Christianity has always been historically understood. Dr. Stephen Robinson provides the Mormon answer to the question whether Mormons are Christians: "Latter-day Saints do not seek to be accepted as historically 'orthodox' Christians or as Evangelicals. We are neither."[37]

continual revelation and mormon scriptural books

Official Mormon teaching and practices today are based primarily in the continual divine revelations and interpretations of the LDS President and Prophet and only secondarily in Mormonism's four written scriptural books that consist of the Bible (King James Version only), *Book of Mormon*, *Doctrine and Covenants*, and *Pearl of Great Price*.[1]

Continual Revelation

In Mormonism all contemporary experiences of revelation and interpretation by the LDS President and Prophet surpass all past written records of revelation in authority, including the Bible.[2] When today's LDS President and Prophet speaks, Mormons listen very carefully.[3] Joseph Smith made it clear from the start of Mormonism that the authoritative ongoing revelations and interpretations of the LDS President and Prophet alone ultimately establish and determine the official teaching and practices of the LDS Church.[4]

In the Mormon mind, what God communicated in the past—even if identified as Holy Scripture—is always secondary to what God is saying to ordained Mormon apostles and prophets today.[5] Mormons believe that they are divinely guided and directed concerning the straight and narrow road to eternal exaltation of godhood ultimately through the contemporary revelations and interpretations of their President and Prophet. The LDS President and Prophet is the single authorized mediator between God and Mormon leaders and members.

Because of the primacy of contemporary revelation through Mormonism's President and Prophet over all its scriptural books, official LDS doctrine and practices are always dynamic and changeable. Any of the most central LDS beliefs today can be changed or updated at any time. This crucial understanding of the changeable nature of official LDS doctrine is confirmed by Mormonism's ninth Articles of Faith creedal statement, "We believe all that God has revealed, all that He does now reveal, and we believe that He will yet reveal many great and important things pertaining to the Kingdom of God."

Through the contemporary revelations and interpretations of Mormon apostles, nothing precludes the LDS Church from embracing future changes or additions to its doctrine and practices. Most Mormons actually expect that there will be changes and additions in the future.[6] As historically proved in the overturning of *Doctrine and Covenants* revelation endorsing the practice of polygamy and other major changes, what Mormons are obligated to believe and practice today is not necessarily what they will be required to profess and obey tomorrow. As a result of the changing nature of official LDS teaching and practices, individual Mormon certainty in their faith can be only temporarily embraced and sustained, for tomorrow another kind of Mormonism can emerge.

Mormon Scriptural Books

Following the absolute authority of the revelations of the LDS President and Prophet, Mormons' official teaching and practices are contained in their written scriptural books collected under the title *The Standard Works of the Church*. Again, the LDS Standard Works are the Bible (King James Version only), *Book of Mormon*, *Doctrine and Covenants*, and *Pearl of Great Price*.

Although individual Mormons are encouraged to read these scriptural books and receive inspiration from them for their daily lives, it is important to understand that official and authorized LDS interpretations of these books—including the Bible—are determined only by the Mormon Church's top fifteen male apostles and prophets who are currently functioning in the Quorums of the First Presidency and the Twelve Apostles.[7] Dr. Stephen Robinson makes this clear:

> The only official interpretations and applications of these doctrinal sources are those that come to the church over the signatures of the First Presidency or the Quorum of the Twelve Apostles (collectively). All the rest is commentary.[8]

Absolutely no one else in Mormonism—no matter how significant or educated—has the right to officially speak on behalf of the LDS Church. In fact, speaking against the official doctrinal positions and interpretations of the LDS Church can lead to Mormon court trials, disfellowship, and excommunication, something that has happened throughout Mormon history.[9]

The Bible

The LDS Church today primarily uses the 1611 version of the King James Bible that contains interpretative chapter notes composed by Mormon systematic theologian Bruce McConkie.[10] But although Mormonism includes the Bible in its collection of scriptural books, Mormon understanding of the absolute authority of the Bible falls drastically short of the high doctrinal standard of the Christian church. The major difference between Mormonism and Christianity concerning the Bible is rooted in the fact that Mormonism believes that the Bible is corrupt, contains errors, and is missing God-inspired books and truths.[11]

In sharp contrast, Christians hold the Bible up as the chief and only standard of their faith and practice. We believe that the entire written Bible—Old and New Testaments—fully communicates all of God's special revelation to humanity. The Bible is fully accurate and totally reliable in all things.[12]

In Mormonism, the Christian view of the Bible is simply not taught. Mormons consider Christians fools for believing in only the Bible. As the *Book of Mormon*'s 2 Nephi 29:6 reads: "Thou fool, that shall say: A Bible, we have got a Bible, and we need no more Bible."[13] This is what Bruce McConkie writes: "There is no more false or absurd doctrine than the sectarian claim that the Bible contains all of the word of God."[14]

Again, unlike Mormonism, Christianity stands firm that the Bible alone is the ultimate and final authority of faith, practice, and teaching.[15] The most important biblical passage supporting the Christian position concerning the trustworthiness of the Bible is 2 Timothy 3:16: "All Scripture is breathed out by God and profitable for teaching, for reproof, for correction, and for training in righteousness."

Christians believe that the Bible is the written Word of God. Mormonism's eighth Articles of Faith creedal statement, however, emphasizes that the Bible is the Word of God only as far as it is correctly translated. The bottom line for Mormonism, as previously stated, is that the Bible is authoritative only as it is understood and interpreted by the Mormon apostles and prophets. Dr. Robert Millet writes:

> The declaration, clarification, and interpretation of doctrine for the church as a whole rest with the presiding councils of the church, the First Presidency and the Quorum of the Twelve Apostles.[16]

The Bible Is Corrupt and Filled with Errors

Although Mormons do not believe that the Bible is totally unworthy or nonvaluable, they do believe that God's original revelation has not been soundly preserved through the centuries, that it contains errors, and that its contents have been badly altered and corrupted.[17] The LDS Church believes not only that the Bible contains numerous errors,[18] but also that many God-inspired truths and books have been taken away[19] or excluded[20] from the original Bible by apostate Christians.[21] The LDS Church believes that several inspired books are not in the Bible that should be, and that other "God-breathed" writings that once existed are now missing.[22] Mormonism states that these "lost books" were probably destroyed or excluded by the apostate Christian church.[23] As a result, the Bible today is a fundamentally incomplete Bible.

Since it is corrupt and contains errors, the Bible is functionally subordinate and fully subject to clarification and revision by the *Book of Mormon*, *Doctrines and Covenants*, and *Pearl of Great Price*.

Joseph Smith's Revision of the Bible

One of the strongest proofs that Mormonism does not believe the Bible is complete or trustworthy is the fact that Mormon founder Joseph Smith in the summer of 1830 began to write his own inspired revision of the Old and New Testaments. Since Joseph Smith believed that many plain and precious truths were missing from the Bible,[24] he claimed that God had instructed him to publish an accurate and fully revised version of the Bible. Today, this is known as the *Joseph Smith Translation* (JST).

Actually, it is very misleading to identify Joseph Smith's revision of the Bible as an authentic translation. It certainly was not. The word *translation* indicates that he used original texts and ancient languages. Instead, Smith makes it clear that his revision of the Bible was accomplished through the power of the Holy Spirit and not by scholarly interpretation. He claimed that God's miraculous guidance enabled him to correct, delete, and add words and whole passages to the Bible.[25] This is how the official LDS *Doctrine and Covenants Student Manual* describes the process:

> Joseph Smith went through all the Bible, dictating to a scribe changes, deletions, or additions, but he did not complete a revision of the entire Bible. He never considered what he had accomplished as ready for publication, and he probably would have made many more corrections had he lived longer.[26]

Joseph Smith's revision of the Bible was started, but it was never published during his lifetime. The manuscript of his Bible revisions and additions was kept by his widow Emma Smith, who refused to follow Brigham Young to Utah after Smith's death, and helped to start the Reorganized Church of Latter Day Saints under the leadership of her son. The Reorganized Church published the JST for the first time in 1867.[27]

Although Mormonism has not included the JST in its scriptural books, it does claim that Joseph Smith's translation is truly inspired, and that it does restore to the Bible many plain and precious truths that had been lost or excluded by apostate Christianity.[28] Yet no ancient manuscripts reveal that the content that Joseph Smith and the LDS Scriptures have attempted to restore to the Bible ever appeared in the original biblical texts in the first place. In fact, Dr. Craig Blomberg, distinguished New Testament professor at Denver Seminary, affirms that "more than 97 percent of the New Testament and over 90 percent of the Old Testament can be reconstructed beyond any measure of reasonable doubt."[29] Dr. Blomberg goes further in his absolute support for the trustworthiness of the Bible:

> None of the ancient manuscripts support the contention that the type of "restorations" that the Joseph Smith translation or the uniquely LDS Scriptures make were ever in the original biblical texts. Neither do any ancient manuscripts exist to support the claim the early church left out entire books from the Bible that would have included distinctively LDS doctrine.[30]

How Do Mormons Read the Bible?

How a person approaches and reads the Bible reveals his or her real trust in its completeness, authenticity, and inspiration. Unlike Christians, who believe that the Bible is the sole primary authority of God's revelation and truth, Mormons read and interpret the Bible only through the filter of the LDS scriptural books and leaders:

> Just as traditional Christianity has no hesitation in viewing the events and teachings of the Old Testament through the lenses of the New Testament, so Latter-day Saints do not hesitate to read the Bible through the lenses of the *Book of Mormon*, modern scripture, and the words of living apostles and prophets.[31]

Book of Mormon

Mormonism places much more certainty and authority in the *Book of Mormon* than it does in the Bible.[32] Mormons emphasize that the *Book of Mormon* is more accurate and trustworthy than the Bible because it is free of errors and contains the fullness of the gospel.[33] The thirteenth Mormon President and Prophet, Ezra Taft Benson, reveals how the LDS Church elevates the *Book of Mormon* over the Bible:

> The Bible sits on the pulpit of hundreds of different religious sects. The *Book of Mormon*, the record of Joseph, verifies and clarifies the Bible. It removes stumbling blocks, it restores many plain and precious things.[34]

The Historical Story of the Book of Mormon

Surprisingly, unlike the *Doctrine and Covenants*, and the *Pearl of Great Price*, the *Book of Mormon* contains very little uniquely LDS doctrine. The primary purpose of the *Book of Mormon* is to provide a historical record of several groups of Old Testament Israelites who supposedly migrated to and lived on the American continent.

The first American migration story told in the *Book of Mormon*[35] concerns a group of Israelites called the *Jaredites*, named after their leader, Jared. The Jaredites supposedly came to America at the time the tower of Babel was being built in approximately 2200 BC. Although very hard to even imagine, the Jaredites supposedly left the Middle East in eight barges that were illuminated by divinely powered, glowing rocks.[36] They drifted the ocean for 344 days until they arrived on the eastern shore of Central America, and grew into a society of millions of people, who spread throughout the Americas until they died off in approximately 400 to 500 BC.[37]

Most of the *Book of Mormon*, however, focuses on the offspring of a Jewish prophet named Lehi and his family, who escaped Jerusalem during the period of the Babylonian captivity in approximately 600 BC. The prophet Lehi is said to have received a revelation from God, telling him and his family, including his four sons, Laman, Lemuel, Sam, and Nephi, to flee Israel and go to an unknown land.

According to the *Book of Mormon* story, Lehi and his family traveled for eight years through the wilderness, probably the Arabian Peninsula, until they apparently came to the Red Sea coast. It is said that they built a ship there.[38] Similar to the biblical story of Noah, Lehi's family and sons, consisting of no more than twenty people, sailed from the Red Sea across the Indian and Pacific Oceans until they landed somewhere in Central or South America.

On the American continent, the Lehi family multiplied and prospered from 600 BC to approximately AD 400. They allegedly constructed many buildings and a temple similar to the size and glory of Solomon's temple.[39] Mormons also say that when Jesus spoke about "other sheep" in John 10:16—"I have other sheep that are not of this fold. I must bring them also, and they will listen to my voice. So there will be one flock, one shepherd"—he was speaking about the Jewish descendants of Lehi who inhabited America. But no Christian Bible teachers affirm this very speculative interpretation.

As the *Book of Mormon* story unfolds, it reveals that the descendants of Lehi separated into two warring nations known as the righteous, light-skinned Nephites led by the youngest son, Nephi, and the wicked, dark-skinned Lamanites led by the oldest son, Laman.[40] In fact, most of the narrative of the *Book of Mormon* is about conflicts and wars between the Nephite and Lamanite nations.

The Last Great American Battle

Most of the individual book of Mormon, the thirteenth book within the collective *Book of Mormon*, tells the bloody story of the American conflicts between the Nephites and Lamanites over the course of approximately a thousand years. This dramatic story comes to a climax around the year AD 421 in their final and greatest war on the hill called Cumorah located in western New York.[41] In the end, the savage Lamanites destroyed the Nephites. Though the idea is completely unsubstantiated by DNA or any other historical evidence, Mormons claim that the descendants of the Lamanites are today's American Indians.[42]

Mormons claim that the history of these early American Hebrew civilizations was written on gold tablets and that Mormon, the Nephite prophet and warrior, gave them to his son Moroni prior to the last great battle.[43] During the final war, Mormon was killed and Moroni, the last living Nephite, went into hiding.

Before Moroni died, he buried these gold tablets on the New York Hill Cumorah, where they remained untouched for fourteen hundred years until unearthed by Joseph Smith. As explained in chapter 1, it is claimed that Joseph Smith was given the *Book of Mormon* gold tablets by the angel Moroni, translated them, and had them published in 1830.

Another Testament of Jesus Christ

The most startling event in the *Book of Mormon* for Christians is the supposed appearance of Jesus Christ among the Nephites in America after his resurrection.[44] To emphasize this American appearance, the LDS Church in 1982 added the subtitle *Another Testament of Jesus Christ* to the *Book of Mormon*. Mormonism now calls the *Book of Mormon* the fifth Gospel, placing it alongside the four biblical Gospels of Matthew, Mark, Luke, and John.

Is the Book of Mormon True?

Because not a single person, place, or event unique to the *Book of Mormon* has been proved to have existed,[45] Mormons emphasize that a subjective heart experience—what they call a burning in the bosom[46]—proves the authenticity and truth of the *Book of Mormon*. For the Latter-day Saints, it is simply a matter of faith—a witness of the spirit—not objective facts, that proves the *Book of Mormon*'s authenticity. The LDS Church exhorts people to study the *Book of Mormon* and claims that they will feel its power and know its divinity.[47] Mormonism highlights Moroni 10:4 in encouraging people to read the *Book of Mormon*:

> When ye shall receive these things, I would exhort you that ye would ask God, the Eternal Father, in the name of Christ, if these things are not true; and if ye shall ask with a sincere heart, with real intent, having faith in Christ, he will manifest the truth of it unto you, by the power of the Holy Ghost.

Yet a close examination of the objective historical and archaeological evidence and the internal content of the *Book of Mormon* will quickly dampen any subjective feelings and impulses that a person may have. Any archaeological scholar will affirm that absolutely no physical evidence in America substantiates with scholarly integrity that early American civilizations of millions of people ever existed as described in the *Book of Mormon*—unlike the evidence of biblical times in the Middle East.

Initially, Mormonism believed much of the *Book of Mormon* historical stories actually took place in upper New York, around the region of the Hill Cumorah, where the gold plates were claimed to have been unearthed by Joseph Smith. But because of the total lack of archaeological or historical evidence that this was true, Mormons are now attempting to identify the ancient Mayan ruins located in southern Mexico and Central America as a possible geographical alternative.[48] In fact, LDS travel agencies even promote tours of the *Book of Mormon* lands in Mexico and Central America.

In the end, however, all the LDS archaeological and geographical claims are simply guesswork. This leaves the so-called historical events described in the *Book of Mormon* in significant question and under real suspicion. Even the Smithsonian Institution declares that there is absolutely no direct connection between the archaeology of the New World and the story of the *Book of Mormon*.[49] As someone who has studied the historical-geographical context of the Bible in Israel for one year and has traveled extensively throughout the land of Turkey for almost two decades, I can attest that the biblical narrative—in contrast to that of the *Book of Mormon*[50]—can be strongly substantiated by hard geographical and archaeological evidence.

Dr. Craig Blomberg also throws great doubt on the authenticity of the content of the *Book of Mormon*, stating that much of its historical context fits in the religious climate and theological concerns of the early 1800s, not during the time that it claims to have occurred:

> The *Book of Mormon* is full of the widespread use, supposedly written in Old Testament times, of New Testament doctrines, language, concepts and even specific verses.[51]

One of the great theological flaws in Mormonism is its Christianizing of the Old Testament.

Doctrine and Covenants

The *Doctrine and Covenants* is primarily the collection of Joseph Smith's revelations and inspired declarations that were supposedly received from God.[52] Intriguingly, the *Doctrine and Covenants* contains historical organizational sections that are very similar to the prophet Muhammad's revelations that were collected in Islam's Qur'an. For Mormonism, the importance of the revelations in the *Doctrine and Covenants* cannot be overemphasized, for they contain many of the unique doctrines of the LDS Church.[53]

The *Doctrine and Covenants* has gone through several revisions over the years.[54] Joseph Smith began selecting and collecting his revelations in the summer of 1830. His first sixty-five revelations were initially published in Independence, Missouri, in 1833 under the title *Book of Commandments for the Government of the Church of Christ*. As Joseph Smith received more visions and revelations, a revised and enlarged compilation was published in Kirtland, Ohio, in 1835 and 1876 as the *Doctrine and Covenants of the Church of Latter-day Saints*. Today's 1990 authorized version of the *Doctrine and Covenants* contains 138 revelations or sections plus the two official LDS declarations ending the practice of polygamy in 1890, and allowing worthy black males to enter the LDS priesthoods in 1978. The *Doctrine and Covenants*, not the *Book of Mormon*, contains most of the primary doctrines that are totally unique to the LDS Church.

Pearl of Great Price

The LDS scriptural volume *Pearl of Great Price*[55] is only approximately sixty pages in length. It is a diverse collection of translations, narrations, and revelations written by Joseph Smith from 1830 to 1842. Over the years, several revisions, subtractions, and additions have been made to the *Pearl of Great Price* collection.

The first collection of Joseph Smith's writings carrying the title *Pearl of Great Price* was completed in 1851 by Mormon Elder Franklin D. Richards. This collection continued to grow in use and became an official LDS scriptural book on October 10, 1880. Today, the *Pearl of Great Price* contains the book of Moses, the book of Abraham, the Prophet Joseph Smith's revisionist translation of Matthew chapter 24, Joseph Smith—History, and the thirteen LDS Articles of Faith.

The Book of Moses

The book of Moses is a small excerpt from Joseph Smith's so-called translation of the early chapters of the book of Genesis, which he began in June 1830.[56] Its eight chapters incorporate teachings that were supposedly lost from the Bible that give additional information about the plan of salvation, the creation of the earth, and the Lord's dealings with Adam and Enoch.

The Book of Abraham

The book of Abraham is Joseph Smith's translation of an Egyptian papyrus manuscript that he purchased in 1835. It contains five short chapters with three facsimiles and explanations. Although the book was originally written in Egyptian, Smith claimed that through his God-given supernatural abilities he discovered that they contained extrabiblical writings of the patriarch Abraham in his own handwriting while he lived in Egypt (Gen. 12:10–20). The translation of these so-called writings of Abraham was initially published in 1842 in the city of Nauvoo, Illinois.[57]

The book of Abraham contains several uniquely LDS doctrines, such as the plurality of gods, the preexistence of humans, and the organization of the world by several gods out of existing matter. The book of Abraham was also used to exclude male blacks from the Mormon priesthoods.

Since the original papyri had apparently disappeared, the LDS Church claimed that the book of Abraham was a direct translation by Joseph Smith, who had used an Egyptian alphabet and grammar that the LDS Church had in its possession. In 1966, however, the Mormon world was rocked when some of the book of Abraham's original papyri were discovered at New York's Metropolitan Museum of Art. The files contained a bill of sale from Emma Smith, Joseph Smith's widow.[58]

After a thorough examination of the papyri and the three facsimiles contained in the book of Abraham, it was authoritatively declared by Egyptologists that the present content in the book of Abraham has nothing at all to do with the original papyri. Actually, the facsimiles and papyri turned out to be pagan Egyptian funerary documents.[59]

Now that it is a proven fact that the LDS book of Abraham has no relationship at all to the Egyptian papyri purchased by Joseph Smith back in 1835, Mormonism now states that Smith did not really translate the extant papyri, but simply used them to obtain supernatural revelation from God. The unfolding saga of the book of Abraham affirms that Mormons embrace their scriptural books—including the *Book of Mormon*—not based on historical authenticity but through an irrational faith.[60]

Joseph Smith—Matthew

Joseph Smith claimed in *Doctrine and Covenants* 45:60–61 that God called him to begin his revision of the New Testament. This section of the *Pearl of Great Price* contains Joseph Smith's revision of Matthew 23:39–24:5 in which he adds material concerning the second coming of Jesus Christ.

Joseph Smith—History

Joseph Smith—History contains excerpts from his official testimony and history of the LDS Church, which he published in 1842 in Nauvoo, Illinois.[61] It contains his version of the First Vision, the Moroni visits, the receiving and translating of the *Book of Mormon* gold plates, and the restoration of the Aaronic Priesthood.

The Thirteen Articles of Faith

The Articles of Faith of the Church of Jesus Christ of Latter-day Saints are thirteen short, concise creedal statements of basic beliefs and doctrines of Mormonism that were written by Joseph Smith and published on March 1, 1842.[62] The LDS Articles of Faith appear as Appendix 1.

THE WORLDVIEW
OF MORMONISM

ormonism and Christianity advocate two deeply contrasting and conflicting worldviews.[1] As Fuller Theological Seminary President Richard Mouw correctly states, "At
the heart of our continuing disagreements, I am convinced,
are the very basic worldview issues."[2] Dr. Stephen Robinson
makes the same general point: "The real sticking point is not
what the LDS think about Christ and his gospel, but rather
the different ontological frame or view of the nature of the
universe into which the Mormons fit the gospel."[3]

James Sire, in *The Universe Next Door*, defines a worldview
as "a set of presuppositions which we hold about the basic
make-up of our world."[4] A worldview is a view of total reality
that is developed by the use of words and concepts in order to
create a coherent frame of reference for all beliefs, thoughts,
and actions.

Essentially, a worldview is our answer to the ultimate
questions of life: What is primary reality, the really real?

What is the nature of external reality, the world around us? What is a human being? What happens to a person at death? Why is it possible to know anything at all? How do we know what is right and wrong? What is the meaning of human history?[5]

It is no accident that the official LDS Web site declares that Mormonism, as the real restored truth, provides answers to life and worldview questions such as these:[6] What's the purpose of my life? Where did I come from? Did I exist before this life? Could a young farm boy really have seen God? Is motherhood part of God's plan? Will I be with my family after death?

Mormonism is much more than just another religion; it is a full-fledged worldview. As the official Web site reveals, Mormons teach a totally different perception concerning the nature of God, the pre-creation universe of eternal realities, the origins of our world, the nature of humanity, and the eternal potential of humans to become gods. In fact, the worldview constructed and promoted by Mormonism mirrors several aspects of ancient paganism, Egyptian and Greek mythology, Hinduism, and New Age, and is foreign and destructive to a biblical Judeo-Christian worldview. As Dr. Jim Adams writes:

> In some significant ways the traditional LDS positions hark back to the pagan views of ancient Israel's Near Eastern neighbors—views that the Old Testament patriarchs, prophets, and psalmists intentionally rejected in light of the revelation they received from the one true and living God.[7]

The Primordial World of Mormonism

The primordial[8] worldview—the original pre-creation order of the universe—of Mormonism is complex and difficult for Christians to understand because it teaches that before creation God lived in a multifaceted universe of coeternal realities composed of eternal laws, intelligences or minds, spirits, and physical matter.[9] In Mormonism, all existence finds its origin in the primordial realm.[10] Mormonism teaches that God eternally existed within an uncreated environment of numerous elements of a preexisting universe.

Eternal Laws and Principles

According to Mormonism—in sharp contrast to the Christian view that God is absolutely and totally above all things—everything in the universe is ultimately governed by eternal transcendent laws and principles.[11] In accordance with this perspective, God himself is also governed by law. In fact, as explained more fully in chapter 7, the Father, Jesus, and the Holy Spirit all progressed into godhood by obeying eternal laws. As a result, since God must work only through natural law to accomplish his purposes, he cannot act from outside or above the realm of nature.[12]

Eternal Intelligences and Spirits

Other uncreated primordial elements existing in the universe for Mormons are eternal divine intelligences.[13] Mormonism teaches that the intelligence—the irreducible mind-part of humans—is eternal, as affirmed by the *Doctrine and Covenants*:

> Man was in the beginning with God. Intelligence, or the light of truth, was not created or made, neither indeed can be. All truth (intelligence) is independent in that sphere in which God has placed it, to act for itself, as all intelligence also; otherwise there is no existence. The glory of God is intelligence, or, in other words, light and truth.[14]

Joseph Smith elaborates in his famous King Follett sermon:

> The mind or the intelligence which man possesses is co-equal with God himself. The intelligence of spirits had no beginning;

neither will it have an end. That is good logic. That which has a beginning may have an end. There never was a time when there were not spirits; for they are co-equal with our Father in heaven. . . . God never had the power to create the spirit of man at all. God himself could not create himself. Intelligence is eternal and exists upon a self-existent principle.[15]

These eternal minds or intelligences are identified by Mormons as the primal component of every human, angel, or god.[16] Mormonism teaches that the eternal mind or intelligent component of every human has the natural capability and potential to grow in knowledge and power until he or she progresses into the glorified state of godhood. For Mormons, this means that humans have the potential to become fully equal with God.

According to Mormonism, because the human spirit[17] proceeds from the existence of these eternal minds or intelligences,[18] the human spirit is not literally created by God. Every human spirit once existed as a divine intelligence before becoming a spirit-offspring of heavenly Father God and his wife. The human mind or spirit has no beginning and will have no end.[19]

Eternal Matter

Another rather surprising teaching of Mormonism is the belief that all physical matter is also eternal, and that it is simply a variation and a denser form of eternal spirit.[20] Joseph Smith declared that God revealed to him that all spirit is actually matter. According to Smith's revelation in *Doctrine and Covenants* 131:7–8:

> There is no such thing as immaterial matter. All spirit is matter, but it is more fine or pure, and can only be discerned by purer eyes. We cannot see it; but when our bodies are purified we shall see that it is all matter.[21]

Mormonism actually emphasizes that the existence of eternal matter is being proved by modern physics.[22]

Many Worlds and Many Gods

Another very puzzling primordial position of Mormonism for Christians is the belief that many inhabited worlds and planets existed before God created our world, as emphasized in the *Pearl of Great Price*'s book of Abraham 3:1–10. Mormonism also believes that these innumerable worlds or kingdoms[23] were also inhabited by gods. This is what Brigham Young, the second Mormon President and Prophet, states:

> How many Gods there are, I do not know. But there never was a time when there were not Gods and worlds, and when men were not passing through the same ordeals [mortality] that we are now passing through. That course has been from all eternity, and it is and will be to all eternity.[24]

Brigham Young even goes further and declares that there were not only many gods on these planets, but also multiple redeemers:

> Every earth has its redeemer, and every earth has its tempter; and every earth, and the people thereof, in their turn and time, receive all that we receive, and pass through all the ordeals that we are passing through.[25]

Although Mormonism does not like the word *polytheism* because it too closely reflects a pagan worldview, there is no doubt that Latter-day Saints believe in the eternal reality of a plurality of gods.[26]

Mormonism also believes that Jesus Christ under the direct authority of Father God created not only this earth but also many other worlds for future humans who would progress into gods to inhabit and fill with spirit-children.[27]

Gods Who Organized the World

In opposition to every branch and denomination of Christianity, Mormonism promotes a theory that a council of gods[28] organized the universe out of independent eternal physical matter instead of creating the world "out of nothing."[29] Joseph Smith, in his famous 1844 King Follett funeral sermon during a church conference near the end of his life, expounded on the idea that God organized the universe out of preexisting chaotic matter:

> You ask the learned doctors why they say the world was made out of nothing, and they will answer, "Doesn't the Bible say he created the world?" They infer, from the word create, that it must have been made out of nothing. Now, the word create came from the word baurau, which does not mean to create out of nothing; it means . . . to organize the world out of chaos—chaos matter, which is element, and in which dwells all the glory. Element had an existence from the time He had. The pure principles of element . . . can never be destroyed . . . ; they may be organized and reorganized, but not destroyed. They had no beginning, and can have no end.[30]

This LDS doctrine is made clear by Brigham Young:

> To assert that the Lord made this earth out of nothing is preposterous and impossible. God never made something out of nothing.[31]

If God simply organized the world, as taught by Mormonism, then God does not actually transcend the natural universe, but is immanent within it. According to Mormonism, God oversaw the organization of this world, but is not the single infinite and absolute Creator of the physical universe as taught in Christianity. What is even more confusing is that the LDS scriptural book *Pearl of Great Price* states that many gods participated in the organization of our universe:

They went down at the beginning, and they, that is, the Gods, organized and formed the heavens and the earth.[32]

God Created the World

The biblical doctrine of creation is indispensable to a distinctively theistic and God-centered worldview and perception of reality. Genesis 1:1—"In the beginning, God created the heavens and the earth"—is the first verse in the Bible, and how a person understands this verse will significantly shape every other facet of his or her perception of ultimate reality. This is why creation is an essential truth for Christians. Christians maintain that God alone is the absolute Creator of every element in the physical universe.

A biblical Christian worldview is founded on the belief that God created all universal reality out of nothing. The God of the Bible is the first cause of all things, and before creation only God existed. As a result, all major branches of Christianity—Protestant, Eastern Orthodox, and Roman Catholic—maintain the total distinction between the Creator and physical creation.

It is important to understand that the biblical doctrine of creation out of nothing is what fundamentally distinguishes the nature of the Judeo-Christian view of God from the multitude of ancient Near Eastern religions and Hellenistic philosophical and mythological systems of classical Greece, which assumed that the world had been formed out of eternally preexisting matter.[33]

One Happy Heavenly Family

Now let's move from Mormonism's perspective of the primordial world to its specific belief in human preexistence. Although it is claimed that our remembrance of this pre-life is veiled from us today, Mormon literature tells an elaborate and detailed story of the premortal existence of a happy heavenly family of which we were all a part. We all lived together for potentially billions of years in a state of total happiness and eternal closeness[34] on a planet near a planet-star named Kolob.[35] Latter-day Saints teach the literal fatherhood of God and the brotherhood of humanity.[36]

Bizarrely to the ears of Christians, Mormonism even believes that animals were also preexistent in spirit form,[37] as the *Book of Mormon* Moses 3 states: "they were all created as spirit entities in preexistence." This is what the *Encyclopedia of Mormonism* teaches concerning animals:

> Latter-day Saints believe that animals, like humans, have spirits, in the form of their bodies (Doctrine and Covenants 77:2). Like humans and plants, animals were created first as spirits in heaven and then physically on earth (Moses 3:5). Mortal and subject to death, animals will be saved through the atonement of Christ. The Prophet Joseph Smith taught that animals will be found in heaven, in myriad forms, from myriad worlds, enjoying eternal felicity, and praising God in languages God understands.[38]

This family story of preexistence is very hard for Christians to reconcile because we base our worldview and perception of all reality primarily on the Bible. Yet it is at least reassuring that Mormons admit that their belief in a preexistent heavenly family originates mainly in modern LDS revelation and not in the teaching of the Bible.

The Heavenly Parents

According to Mormonism, all humans today are the literal spirit-children and offspring of heavenly parents before the creation of the world.[39] For example, when Mormons pray to their Father God, they believe that they are communicating with their literal heavenly father.[40] Dr. Stephen Robinson writes:

> Latter-day Saints believe in the literal fatherhood of God and the brotherhood of humanity. . . . All men and women were his spiritual offspring in pre-mortal existence.[41]

Mormonism rarely mentions a heavenly Mother,[42] but based on the Mormon teaching of eternal Celestial marriage and procreation, it is logical to conclude that Mormonism believes God the Father is married to an eternal wife or possibly to many wives. According to Bruce McConkie:

> Implicit in the Christian verity that all men are the spirit children of an *Eternal Father* is the usually unspoken truth that they are also the offspring of an *Eternal Mother.* An exalted and glorified Man of Holiness (Moses 6:57) could not be a Father unless a Woman of like glory, perfection, and holiness was associated with him as a Mother. The begetting of children makes a man a father and a woman a mother whether we are dealing with man in his mortal or immortal state. This doctrine that there is a *Mother in Heaven* was affirmed in plainness by the First Presidency of the Church (Joseph F. Smith, John R. Winder, and Anthon H. Lund) when, in speaking of pre-existence and the origin of man, they said that "man, as a spirit, was begotten and born of heavenly parents. . . ."[43]

Mormons teach that God's spirit-children will also have their own spirit-children as gods if they are eternally exalted to the highest level of the Celestial heaven, as we will explore in more detail in chapter 8.[44]

The Heavenly Spirit-Children

Because God the Father and Mother possess physical bodies, Mormonism believes they are able to give birth to billions of spirit-children. It is at this time of birthing that eternal intelligences or minds are clothed with spiritual bodies and become personages of spirit. And when these eternal intelligences are birthed, they take on the beginning of their human ego as a conscious identity[45]—although some Mormons today assume that a preexistent intelligence is a conscious and self-aware person even before spirit-birth. No Mormon sources explain exactly how the births of these spirit-children actually take place, but it seems logical that since eternal marriage is required to have spirit-children, then bodily sex is experienced and heavenly mothers experience a birth process similar to that on earth. Yet this remains an unexplained and unclear Mormon doctrine.

Mormons call the preexistence of all human spirits the "First Estate" and strongly reject the idea that individual spirits are created at the moment of conception or at birth.[46] They believe spirit-children have lived for an indefinite amount of time in the presence of their Father God before they come to earth to inhabit their earthly physical bodies or tabernacles.

All spirit-children are individual entities—male and female—with distinct personalities and characters. This is why Mormons today address other LDS members with the title of *Brother* or *Sister*, along with the individual's last name (Brother Jones or Sister Smith). Dr. Robert Millet makes this clear:

Latter-day Saints believe that men and women are literally the spirit sons and daughters of God, that we lived in a premortal existence before birth, that we grew and expanded in that "first estate" (*Pearl of Great Price*, Abraham 3:36), all in preparation for this "second estate." In that world men and women were separate and distinct spirit personages, had consciousness, volition, maleness and femaleness, and moral agency. They developed and matured according to our adherence to God's eternal law, and in spite of the fact that we walked and talked with God, it was necessary for them to exercise faith in God's plan for ultimate salvation of his children. The Latter-day Saints believe that God is literally the Father of our spirits, that we inherit from him divine capacities, the seeds of godliness. In the long expanse of time before we were born into mortality, the spirit sons and daughters of God developed talents, strengths, and capacities. In a sense, no two persons remained alike.[47]

In drastic contrast to the belief that all humans are literal preexistent spirit-children, Christians emphasize the clear biblical teaching that we are children of God through faith and spiritual adoption when we put our faith in Jesus Christ: "for in Christ Jesus you are all sons of God, through faith" (Gal. 3:26); "This means that it is not the children of the flesh who are the children of God, but the children of the promise are counted as offspring" (Rom. 9:8); "But to all who did receive him, who believed in his name, he gave the right to become children of God, who were born, not of blood nor of the will of the flesh nor of the will of man, but of God" (John 1:12–13).

Not one branch or denomination of Christianity has ever taught Mormonism's idea of the preexistence of humanity. Not a single one. There is absolutely no theological commonality between Christianity and Mormonism when it comes to human preexistence.

Mormon Angels as Spirit-Children

Again, in total distinction from Christianity, Mormonism believes that angels are not uniquely created beings distinct from humans, as taught in the Bible.[48] Latter-day Saints have numerous twists on the identity of angels.[49] Parley Pratt, a Mormon apostle, wrote: "Gods, angels, and men are all of one species, one race, one great family."[50]

Mormonism teaches that angels can be spirit-children who have not yet taken on bodies in mortality.[51] For example, the

LDS Church believes that Adam preexisted as the archangel Michael, and that the angel Gabriel was born into the world as Noah.[52] Some angels are humans who have completed their mortal existence and minister from paradise in the spirit-world, such as Moroni and John the Baptist. Mormons also believe that some angels are those who lived on earth but were not eternally married in the temple and so did not qualify for eternal life and exaltation. As a result, their eternal destiny is one of being ministering angels and not exalted gods.[53]

Good and Bad Spirit-Children

Mormonism emphasizes that all spirit-children must live in obedience to the eternal laws and principles of ultimate reality through the moral agency of free will. LDS theology is strongly based in what Mormons call moral agency. This is how the LDS official Web site defines Mormonism's view of moral agency:

> Agency is the ability and privilege God gives us to choose and to act for ourselves. Agency is essential in the plan of salvation. Without it, we would not be able to learn or progress or follow the Savior. With it, we are "free to choose liberty and eternal life, through the great Mediator of all men, or to choose captivity and death, according to the captivity and power of the devil" (2 Nephi 2:27).[54]

This stress on free will undergirds Mormonism's absolute commitment to a form of Arminian theology.[55] It might even be better and more accurate to speak of Mormonism's commitment to libertarian free will as a form of Pelagianism.[56]

Mormons believe that during this premortal existence, each person developed a unique identity and increased in his or her spiritual capabilities. Through a moral free will, each spirit-child was able to make right or wrong decisions.

Somewhat similar to the teaching of reincarnation that results in Hinduism's present caste system, Mormonism advocates that the way in which preexistent spirit-children lived in their premortal existence also has a direct correlation to their condition of life on earth. For example, Mormonism teaches that many obedient spirit-children in the preexistence became members of the nation of Israel:

> For Mormons, Israel is an eternal people. Members of that chosen race first gained their inheritance with the faithful in the pre-mortal life. Israel was a distinct people in pre-existence. Many of the valiant and noble spirits in that first estate were chosen, elected, and foreordained to be born into the family of Jacob, so as to be natural heirs of all the blessings of the gospel.[57]

Mormonism has also taught that there were disobedient preexisting spirit-children. One such disobedient child was Cain, who entered earthly mortality with dark skin, as Mormon Prophet Joseph Fielding Smith made clear:

> There is a reason why one man is born black and with other disadvantages, while another is born white with great advantages. The reason is that we once had an estate before we came here, and were obedient, more or less, to the laws that were given us there. Those who are faithful in all things there received greater blessings here, and those who were not faithful received less.[58]

Although this view has not been officially denounced, many Mormons today no longer seem to emphasize or directly teach their past "curse of Cain" doctrine. Apparently on the basis of the Mormon belief that male blacks were disobedient preexistent spirit-children, they were not allowed to hold office in the LDS priesthood.[59] A new revelation, however, was received in 1978 by LDS President and Prophet Spencer W. Kimball that changed Mormonism's official position. Latter-day Saints now allow blacks to become authorized and ordained LDS priests. But as far as I am aware, they have not rejected their early teaching that how a spirit lives in his or her preexistent life directly determines the person's condition in mortal life.

Bruce McConkie summarizes this general Mormon teaching: "It is only by knowledge of pre-existence that it can be known why some persons are born in one race or caste and some in another,"[60] and "the race and nation in which men are born in this world is a direct result of their pre-existent life."[61]

The Gospel of Eternal Progression into Godhood

As the Mormon story goes, after ages of living as one happy heavenly family, Father God called for a family gathering or council, at which time he presented to his millions of spirit-children the gospel of eternal progression into godhood, the LDS plan of salvation. The heavenly Father's plan would enable his spirit-children to become gods exactly like him. Mormons call the heavenly Father's plan "the plan of salvation,"[62] "the great plan of happiness,"[63] or "the plan of redemption."[64]

This Mormon salvation plan is identified as the fullness of the gospel, and includes creation, the fall of Adam and Eve, the atonement of Jesus Christ, and obedience to all the laws, ordinances, and doctrines of the LDS Church. Essential to this gospel plan is human moral agency, the ability for everyone to freely choose and act. Through this salvation plan, humans through obedience are enabled to reach godhood and to have families that last forever.

At this great family council, Father God told his spirit-children that his salvation plan required them to leave their heavenly home and take on physical mortal bodies on earth so that each of them could progress higher into a god, as he had.

But the heavenly Father's son Lucifer—today's Satan—had other ideas.

In defiance of Father God's eternal plan of exaltation, his spirit-son Lucifer rebelled and rejected this plan of salvation, wanting to eliminate the law of choice and obedience.[65] But the firstborn son, Jesus Jehovah, stood up in opposition to Lucifer in favor of Father God. Jesus declared that he would become the Savior, take on a mortal body, and live a sinless life in order that all his brothers and sisters could become gods.[66]

As a result, a major war broke out in the preexistent heavenly family between the followers of Jesus and the followers of Lucifer.[67] Lucifer and his followers fought against the archangel Michael—who would be born Adam on earth—and lost.

In the end, all the heavenly spirit-children had to choose whether they would follow Jesus or Lucifer (Satan). All the spirit-children who followed the heavenly Father and Jesus Christ were permitted to be born on earth in order to experience mortality and progress toward eternal divine exaltation. The spirit-children who rebelled and followed Satan were excommunicated from the heavenly family and cast down to earth without physical bodies, forfeiting their opportunity to progress into gods.[68] Mormons teach that a third of the spirit-children chose to become Lucifer followers. In this light, Mormons identify Satan and demons as their preexistent brothers and sisters who are now in active opposition to the eternal plan of their Father God.

Adam's Role in Mormon Salvation

Adam—who as we have seen was the archangel Michael in preexistence—plays a major role in Mormon salvation, a theological position that is totally foreign to Christianity. In fact, the LDS Church teaches that Adam and Eve's fall was a positive event—a fortunate fall—and a significant salvation strategy of God. Dr. Robert Millet summarizes the Mormon position:

> Mormons believe that Adam and Eve went into the Garden to fall, that their partaking of the forbidden fruit was a necessary step in God's plan for the redemption and happiness of humankind. Though our first parents transgressed the law of God, their partaking opened the way to mortality, to trial and testing to be sure, but to happiness that comes from overcoming.[69]

This is how Dr. Millet defines the fall of Adam in the garden of Eden:

> For Latter-day Saints, the Fall of Adam and Eve was a "fortunate fall," one that introduced mortality and helped to put the Father's plan for the salvation of his children into operation. It was a fall downward but forward.[70]

Although the Latter-day Saints continue to recognize Adam as a redemptive hero for his apparent heroic act of transgression—not sin—in the garden of Eden, this idea is quite different from Brigham Young's apparent Adam-God theory, that is, that Latter-day Saints worship Adam as their Father in heaven. Most Mormons deny this claim as a non-Mormon falsehood.[71] But make no mistake, Mormonism elevates Adam to the highest possible position under the Godhead, as this statement in Bruce McConkie's *Mormon Doctrine* reveals:

> . . . Adam in his proper high place as the pre-existent Michael, the first man and presiding high priest (under Christ) over all the earth for all time, and as the one who will again lead the armies of heaven in the final great war with Lucifer. There is a sense, of course, in which Adam is a god.[72]

Mortal Existence and Attaining Godhood

Now that we understand the Mormon doctrine of human preexistence, what is the purpose of human mortal existence? According to the LDS plan of salvation, when spirit-children are united in bodies through human birth, they begin a lifelong journey of probation, testing, and trials, during which time they learn obedience that they hope will lead them back to Father God in a glorified state of divine exaltation. According to Mormonism, the purpose of earthly mortal existence is to prove obedience to the heavenly Father and to become worthy of eternal exaltation in the highest level of the Celestial kingdom:[73]

> By following our Heavenly Father's plan, you—like all of His children—can someday return to live with Him and with your loved ones. You can have greater peace in this life and eternal joy in the life to come.[74]

Mortal living for Mormons is seen as a school in which they are gods-in-process.[75] Human mortality is a testing and proving ground, a time when a person can prove that he or she is faithful to the heavenly Father's salvation plan. In this light, large Mormon families are not simply an accident. Many Mormons have large families as an act of obedience in order to provide bodies—earthly tabernacles—for the millions of spirit-children waiting to start their mortal journey of progression toward godhood.[76]

GODS AND THE MORMON GOSPEL OF DEIFICATION

ormonism teaches that God was once a human being, and that human beings can become gods.[1] "As man now is, God once was; as God now is, man may become" is for Christians a very startling statement made by Lorenzo Snow—the fifth Mormon President and Prophet.[2] Some Mormons even speak about humans as "Gods in embryo."[3]

President Snow's theological statement is accepted as doctrinal restoration by the majority of Latter-day Saints today. This troubling declaration summarizes for us the official Mormon teaching concerning the past human nature of God, and the future potential for humans to become gods. This chapter will explore one of the deepest theological divides between Christianity and Mormonism concerning the identity and nature of God and man.

The Gods of Mormonism

One of the biggest theological problems between Christianity and Mormonism is Christians' belief in the existence of only one God and the LDS Church's belief in the existence of many gods,[4] as the *Pearl of Great Price*'s Abraham 4:1 states:

> And then the Lord said: Let us go down. And they went down at the beginning, and they, that is the Gods, organized and formed the heavens and the earth.

Bruce McConkie could not be any more clear in this statement:

> There are an infinite number of holy personages, drawn from worlds without number, who have passed on to exaltation and are thus Gods. Indeed, this doctrine of plurality of Gods is so comprehensive and glorious that it reaches out and embraces every exalted personage. Those who attain exaltation are Gods.[5]

Although Mormons do not like to be identified as polytheists—those believing in many gods—because of the direct correlation to paganism,[6] no matter how you spin it, Latter-day Saints affirm and teach a plurality of gods.

Now let's look at how the LDS Church formulates and fits the doctrine of the Godhead—Father, Son, and Holy Spirit—within its multitude of gods that populate innumerable worlds or kingdoms scattered throughout the universe.

The Mormon Godhead

The first LDS Articles of Faith creedal statement, "We believe in God, the Eternal Father, and in His Son, Jesus Christ, and in the Holy Ghost," sounds quite orthodox to Christian ears.

But Mormonism unapologetically rejects and redefines the Christian understanding of the triune nature of God called Trinitarian monotheism, which is fully accepted by Protestants, Roman Catholics, and Eastern Orthodox. Following is a concise definition of the Christian Trinitarian—three-in-one—understanding of the nature of God:

> The Trinitarian concept of God is the Father, Son, and Holy Spirit are the personal, unique, infinite, Creator God. They are not three beings or three Gods, because Trinitarianism firmly embraces monotheism—the belief that there is only one true God. According to orthodox Trinitarianism, there are three distinct persons who together are one being—God.[7]

While all the major branches of Christianity believe that the Father, Son, and Holy Spirit are three distinct persons existing in one indivisible substance, Mormonism teaches and believes that there are three totally separate gods in the Godhead—the Father, Son, and Holy Spirit.[8] These three separate gods are one only in purpose, not one in being or nature.[9] Latter-day Saints reject the Christian belief that God is three coequal persons in one substance or essence, as Dr. Stephen Robinson makes clear in his book *Are Mormons Christians?*:

> If by "the doctrine of the Trinity" one means the doctrine formulated by the councils of Nicaea and Chalcedon and elaborated upon by subsequent theologians and councils—that God is three coequal persons in one substance and essence—then Latter-day Saints do not believe it.[10]

The LDS understanding of the Godhead is not Christian Trinitarianism but Mormon tritheism, that is, the Father, Son, and Holy Spirit are three totally separate gods that progressed and developed into individual deities at different times prior to creation.[11] Bruce McConkie writes:

> Three separate personages—Father, Son, and Holy Ghost—
> comprise the Godhead. As each of these persons is a God, it
> is evident, from this standpoint alone, that a plurality of Gods
> exists.[12]

In fact, the LDS Church describes the Godhead—the Father, Son, and Holy Spirit—more as the supreme heavenly presidency of three gods[13] than as the historically and universally accepted Christian doctrine of the eternal triune nature of one God. On what authoritative basis does Mormonism teach this understanding of the Godhead? Dr. Stephen Robinson tells us:

> We believe this not because it is the clear teaching of the Bible
> but because it was the personal experience of the prophet
> Joseph Smith in his first vision and because the information is
> further clarified for us in modern revelation.[14]

Mormonism's doctrine of the Godhead has absolutely no precedence in the history of the Christian church. For example, during the in-depth theological discussions among Christians concerning the internal nature of God, they never promoted a doctrine of tritheism or belief in three separate gods, as taught in Mormonism today. Early Christians were at all times strict monotheists, believing in one absolute eternal God.[15]

Father Elohim

The Latter-day Saints' understanding of God the Father is central to their view of the Godhead and their faith. Mormonism is thoroughly subordinationist in its theology of the Godhead. In Mormon thinking, Father God—also referred to by the name Elohim—is the primary ruling god in the hierarchy of the Godhead,[16] and the literal father of all spirit-children, including Jesus and the Holy Spirit. Dr. Stephen Robinson affirms this viewpoint rather plainly: "If the Father did not exist, neither the Son nor the Holy Ghost would be God, for their divinity comes through their relationship with the Father."[17]

The Father is the primary god and the principal source of deity. Although the Latter-day Saints refer to Jesus and the Holy Spirit by the term *God*, in actuality the term *God* refers first and foremost to the Father alone.[18] The Father is the "God of Gods."[19] In fact, Joseph Smith called the Father "God the first," Jesus "God the second," and the Holy Spirit "God the third."[20] This seems to be consistent with the Mormon teaching, as will be explained in chapter 8, that God the Father and Jesus will dwell in the highest level of the Celestial kingdom, Jesus will visit the lower Celestial level and Terrestrial kingdoms, and only the Holy Spirit will visit the lowest Telestial kingdom.

The Father is the Supreme Being, the prime source of deity in the Godhead. As spirit-children of the Father, Jesus and the Holy Spirit are sequentially secondary in that they developed into gods after the Father sometime prior to creation. The deity of Jesus and the Holy Spirit then became a reality only through their parent-child relationship with the Father. This raises a very important question: if all of the Father's spirit-children worship him, why don't Jesus and the Holy Spirit do so, since they are also spirit-children? And why do spirit-children worship Jesus and the Holy Spirit, who are fellow spirit-children even if they have progressed into gods?

Based on Mormon theology, the present divine status of the Father, Jesus, and the Holy Spirit is that of earned deity. Even more confusing for Christians is the LDS belief that God the Father himself has and worships a Father God. Joseph Smith clearly states that there is "a God above the Father of our Lord Jesus Christ."[21]

In stark contrast to the teaching of Mormonism, Christians have understood a functional subordination of Jesus to the Father only during his incarnational life and ministry on earth, but we have never advocated an ontological subordination related to the eternal nature and being of the Father and Jesus.[22] This doctrine of Jesus' submission to the Father during his earthly life and ministry is distinctly explained by the apostle Paul in Philippians 2:5–8:

> Have this mind among yourselves, which is yours in Christ Jesus, who, though he was in the form of God, did not count equality with God a thing to be grasped, but made himself nothing, taking the form of a servant, being born in the likeness of men. And being found in human form, he humbled himself by becoming obedient to the point of death, even death on a cross.

In Mormonism, the Father is an exalted man.[23] Joseph Smith called him the *Man of Holiness*[24] who is a physical being with flesh and bones and is not an immaterial spirit.[25] Latter-day Saints maintain a major interpretation twist on what is meant in Genesis 1:26–27 by the statement that man was made in the image of God. Mormons argue that this means that we were created in the physical image of God. Dr. Stephen Robinson writes this concerning humans' being created in God's image: "We take this literally to mean that God has a physical image and that humanity is created in it."[26] According to the official LDS student manual *Doctrines of the Gospel*, God made man in his own image and made the woman in the image of his wife.[27]

Mormons believe that God the Father is "an exalted, glorified, and perfected Man."[28] If we could see God the Father today, he would be in the form of a man.[29] Many Latter-day Saints believe that their literal Father Elohim was once a human man who through obedience and worthiness on another planet progressed and developed into a god.[30] Joseph Smith makes this Mormon view of the nature of God the Father quite clear:

> I will go back to the beginning before the world was, to show what kind of a being God is. What sort of a being was God in

the beginning? God himself was once as we are now, and is an exalted man, and sits enthroned in yonder heavens! That is the great secret. If the veil were rent today, and the great God who holds this world in its orbit, and who upholds all worlds and all things by His power, was to make himself visible,—I say, if you were to see him today, you would see him like a man in form like yourselves in all the person, image, and very form as a man; for Adam was created in the very fashion, image and likeness of God, and received instruction from, and walked, talked and conversed with Him, as one man talks and communes with another. We have imagined and supposed that God was God from all eternity. I will refute that idea, and take away the veil, so that you may see. These are incomprehensible ideas to some, but they are simple. It is the first principle of the gospel to know for a certainty the character of God, and to know that we may converse with Him as one man converses with another, and that He was once a man like us; yea, that God himself, the Father of us all, dwelt on an earth.[31]

Brigham Young University professor Dr. Robert Millet writes:

God our Father was once a mortal, that he lived on an earth, died, was resurrected, and glorified, and grew and developed over time to become the Almighty that he now is. To say this another way, they teach that God is all-powerful and all-knowing, but that he has not been so forever; there was once a time in an eternity past when he lived on an earth like ours.[32]

Jesus Jehovah

In Mormon thinking, Jesus was the first spirit-son born to Father God and his wife or one of his wives.[33] This is why Latter-day Saints identify Jesus as the Son of God and also as their Elder Brother. For Mormons, their Elder Brother Jesus became their Messiah, Redeemer, and Lord.

In Mormonism, Jesus is in the hierarchy of the Godhead a secondary god under Father God. Latter-day Saints believe that Jesus became a god in his preexistence as an obedient spirit-son. Bruce McConkie writes:

> By obedience and devotion to the truth he attained that pinnacle of intelligence which ranked him as a God, as the Lord Omnipotent while yet in his pre-existent state.[34]

Within Mormonism, Jesus is identified as the premortal Jehovah or Yahweh of the Old Testament. Under the direction of the supreme Father God, Jesus organized the worlds,[35] walked in the garden of Eden with Adam and Eve, and was the God of Abraham, Isaac, and Jacob.

The Nameless Holy Spirit

The Holy Spirit is another male child of Father God, and is called a god by Mormons. But unlike the Father and Jesus, who have physical bodies of flesh and bone, the Holy Spirit—or "Holy Ghost," as Mormons like to call him—has only a spirit body in the form of a man. Just as the Father and Jesus can't be omnipresent—present everywhere at one time—because of their physical bodies, neither can the Holy Spirit.[36] For Mormons, the Holy Spirit—a spirit male personage—functions under the direct authority of the Father and Jesus in his roles as comforter, sanctifier, and the revelator. Although they do not seem so prominent and public in the LDS Church today, historical Mormonism believed in and openly practiced spiritual gifts, as stated in the seventh LDS Articles of Faith creedal statement: "We believe in the gift of tongues, prophecy, revelation, visions, healing, interpretation of tongues, and so forth."

The Mormon Gospel of Human Deification

Mormonism teaches that finite humans can actually progress into infinite gods as the Father, Jesus, and the Holy Spirit once did.[37] Mormons proselytize the belief that human deification, or attaining godhood, is in fact the restored LDS gospel message of salvation to the world.[38] This LDS salvation doctrine of the possibility of humans' becoming gods best defines the exclusive teaching of Mormonism, and sets the LDS Church totally apart from all monotheistic faiths, including every branch of historic or contemporary Christianity.[39] This revealing statement from the *Encyclopedia of Mormonism* clarifies the LDS teaching concerning the possibility of humans' becoming gods:

> It is LDS teaching that all the Father's children possess the potential to strive toward the same godhood that the Godhead already has; because in their humanity there is a divinity that is progressing and growing according to the faith, intelligence, and love that abounds in their souls.[40]

And so we must ask the following question: On what authoritative basis can Mormons advocate such an unchristian doctrine? The answer to this question is that Latter-day Saints believe that humans and gods possess the same essential eternal nature.

The Eternal Nature of God and Humans Is the Same

The Mormon teaching concerning human exalted deification or attaining godhood is based on the LDS belief that all humans are of the same species and kind of eternal spirit as God.[41] Although Jews and Christians have always maintained the absolute distinction between God and humans, Dr. Robert Millet emphasizes that Latter-day Saints teach that "man is not of a lower order or different species than God."[42] For Mormons, God and humans are the same species of being or race,[43] and differ only in our degrees of advancement, development, and progress. The *Encyclopedia of Mormonism* makes this LDS teaching clear:

Like Jesus Christ, all mortals live in a state of humiliation, but through the mediation of the Christ they may progress to a state of exaltation. There is no ultimate disparity between the divine and human natures; Joseph Smith asserted that mankind is the same species as God, having been made in God's image and being eternal, with unlimited capacity.[44]

Humans Possess Eternal Intelligences or Spirits

Mormonism teaches that the eternal nature of God and humans is exactly the same and that human spirits originate or are begotten from eternal divine minds or intelligences. In the eternities, our divine intelligences were clothed with spiritual bodies and became personages of spirit. Every human spirit once existed as a divine intelligence before becoming a spirit-offspring of the heavenly Father. The human spirit is not uniquely created by God,[45] but is formed and birthed from eternal existing divine minds or intelligences. They have no beginning, and they will have no end.[46] In this light, Mormonism believes that uncreated eternal intelligence has the innate capability of growing in knowledge and power into god-existence and status.

Becoming Fully God

In Mormonism, the strong distinction that Christians make between the natures of the human and the divine applies only in our present earthly condition of mortality.[47] In fact, the term *human* in Mormonism is relevant only to this earthly life because in future eternity, humans have the potential to become fully equal with God, possessing his divine attributes and abilities.[48] LDS writers claim that the Christian distinction between God and humans is a historical product of Greek philosophy and not the teaching of the Bible.[49] Many Mormons argue that the absolute distinction that Christians believe exists between humans and God is simply a negative by-product of Christianity's being theologically distorted by Hellenistic philosophy.

In other words, the distinction between humans and God is only a temporary and mortal dissimilarity. Humans are different from God only in our fallen earthly condition, but in our exalted and glorified state of exaltation, humans become fully gods. Mormonism teaches that humans can become entirely and completely what God is now, possessing the fullness of God's unique attributes, and engaging fully in all the activities that God does.[50] Dr. Stephen Robinson emphatically states that exalted humans will share both God's communicable and incommunicable attributes:[51]

> Granted there is a gulf between fallen humanity and exalted divinity, but Mormons believe this gulf is bridged in Christ Jesus. In our fallen condition, we are utterly different, but in our saved and glorified state we will be what God is through God's grace, *even in God's so-called incommunicable attributes.* If the redeemed really do become one with the Father and the Son, in the same way that they are one with each other, then how can anyone deny that the redeemed share their divine attributes—even the so-called incommunicable attributes?[52]

In his statement below, Dr. Robinson goes on to further argue for humans' being able to progress fully into gods:

> If the divine can become fully human and then as human be raised up again to be fully God (Phil. 2:6–11), then it is established that what is fully human may also be divine.[53]

In other words—according to Mormon teaching—humans can progress into gods in the fullest sense. Mormons have no theological problems in claiming that the finite can become infinite.[54] In absolute contrast with all branches of Christianity, Mormonism teaches that humans can become "identical in kind" with God in exaltation, as we read in *Doctrine and Covenants* 76:94–95:

> They who dwell in his presence are the church of the Firstborn; and they as they are seen, and know as they are known, having received of his fulness and of his grace; and he makes them equal in power, and in might, and in dominion.

Christian Glorification versus Mormon Deification

Several LDS writers today like to indicate—inadequately—that the early church fathers and the Eastern Orthodox Church actually supported their doctrine of humans' becoming gods.[55] But it is important that we be more accurate than these Mormon writers have been. Let's be clear in our research.

Although some early church fathers and Eastern Orthodox have often spoken about a Christian's eternal hope as deification, divinization, or becoming godlike, they are attempting to describe the Christian's future mystical union with the Trinity.[56] They did not believe or teach that humans could become fully equal with God. There is a significant difference between Christian glorification and the human deification taught in Mormonism. Christians teach eternal human glorification, but not Mormon deification.[57]

Christians advocate that through the eternal grace and power of Jesus Christ we will become "like God" through salvation transformation, which is radically different from the Mormon version of becoming "equal to God." Christians are to be people infused with a great future hope in experiencing the glory of God. God has great eternal blessings in store for everyone who puts their faith and trust in Jesus Christ for salvation. Our confident hope is in God; it is a future hope of a life transformed and glorified by God (Titus 3:7). The biblical hope of human glorification is the anchor of our souls (Heb. 6:19).

Christians are clear and resolved. We are created finite humans who worship a one-of-a-kind eternal God, filled with God's eternal hope and power that enables us to escape the corruption of this evil world (2 Peter 1:4).[58] As followers of Christ, we have hearts set on fire with the future hope of enjoying God for eternity, and we look forward to total transformation, as the apostle John declares:

> Beloved, we are God's children now, and what we will be has not yet appeared; but we know that when he appears we shall be like him, because we shall see him as he is. And everyone who thus hopes in him purifies himself as he is pure (1 John 3:2–3).

Mormon teaching concerning the past human nature of God and future god-potential of humans creates the Grand Canyon divide between Christianity and Mormonism. In contrast with Mormonism, Christianity stands strong in affirming and preserving the total and complete distinction between God and humankind forever (Rom. 1:18–32).

As Christians, we will be "re-created in God's image, perfect in holiness and immortal in nature, with physically resurrected and glorified bodies,"[59] but this does not mean that humans take on God's being and unique attributes or the ability to create or redeem. We will receive all the spiritual blessings of God in Jesus Christ as revealed in Ephesians 1:3–14, but this eternal experience will be quite different from functioning in all the powers of God, as taught in Mormonism. It is unthinkable, repulsive, and even blasphemous to Christians for anyone to spread the teaching that humans can become fully equal to the eternal God we worship.

PART 3

The Salvation of Mormonism

THE HEAVENS AND HELL OF MORMONISM

M ormon teaching concerning the eternal destinations of heaven and hell provides another significant doctrinal divide between Latter-day Saints and Christianity. Christians believe that following the final judgment, heaven and hell are the only two eternal destinations determined by God. Mormonism, however—although it affirms eternal hell—has constructed a complex belief system in three heavenly divisions identified by Joseph Smith as the Celestial, Terrestrial, and Telestial kingdoms that contain various degrees of eternal glory. Mormonism understands these three heavenly kingdoms as representing descending degrees of eternal glory—the Celestial being the highest and the Telestial being the lowest—and compares their divisions of heavenly glories to the natural distinction existing between the brightness of the sun, stars, and moon.

This chapter explores how Mormonism's three kingdoms of glory directly correspond to the general categories of Mormon salvation—universal, partial,[1] and exalted.[2]

The General Categories of Mormon Salvation

It is essential that we first understand what the LDS Church really means by the word *salvation* itself. Otherwise, things can become very confusing and puzzling, especially for Christians. Without this clarity of terminology, Mormon salvation cannot be properly understood and contrasted with biblical salvation in the God-accepted righteousness of Jesus Christ alone.[3]

Universal Salvation

One category of salvation within Mormonism is so-called universal salvation.[4] Clarity and focus are very important when speaking about the Mormon teaching of general or universal salvation. Appealing to 1 Corinthians 15:22, "For as in Adam all die, so also in Christ shall all be made alive," Mormons understand universal salvation as salvation from physical death for everyone.[5] Mormons teach that because of the resurrection of Jesus Christ, all humans will be bodily resurrected from the dead and united with their spirits.

By universal salvation the LDS Church does not mean that everyone will experience the fullness of eternal exaltation in the highest Celestial kingdom, but that every person—whether good or evil—will simply experience bodily resurrection from the dead and receive endless life, nothing more. In Mormonism, immortality itself is salvation from the grave. Through the atonement of Jesus Christ, everyone will receive this gift of immortality.[6]

Christians should be aware that Mormons identify only universal salvation as being *salvation by grace alone*. Humanity's experience of universal salvation from the dead is a total gift from God, and it requires no obedience to LDS gospel covenant laws.[7] When Mormons write or say that they believe in *salvation by grace alone*, they are referring only to universal salvation.

Exalted Salvation

Joseph Smith's vision description of the Celestial kingdom is found in *Doctrine and Covenants* 76:50–70, 92–96. It is imperative to understand that according to Mormonism, the Celestial heavenly kingdom contains three primary levels,[8] and it is only in the highest Celestial level that worthy Mormons will experience exalted salvation and eternal life. It is also essential for Christians to understand that for Mormons the phrase *eternal life* in the Bible refers only to exalted salvation in the highest level of the Celestial kingdom.[9] In exaltation, faithful Mormons experience the fullness of God's life and salvation. The LDS Church identifies *eternal life* as life with and like God. It is God's life.[10] This is how the official LDS Web site defines *eternal life*:

> Eternal life is the phrase used in scripture to define the quality of life that our Eternal Father lives. Eternal life, or exaltation, is to live in God's presence and to continue as families.[11]

For further clarification, as Dr. Robert Millet states below, the words *salvation, exaltation,* and *eternal life* are synonymous in Mormon terminology and salvation theology:

> To possess exaltation is to possess eternal life, to be entitled to the blessings of the highest degree of the celestial kingdom. The word exaltation lays stress upon the elevated and ennobled status of one who qualifies for the society of the redeemed and glorified. Essentially, salvation, exaltation, and eternal life, in their purest sense, are synonymous terms.[12]

All sincere Mormons today focus on exalted fullness in the highest level of the Celestial kingdom as their life's one salvation goal. For Mormons, entrance into the highest Celestial heaven is the ultimate prize of salvation because the highest Celestial kingdom is the true Mormon heaven. Mormons are indoctrinated their whole lives not to settle for any less eternal aspiration or dream. To fall short of earning eternal life and exaltation would be a real sense of personal failure and guilt for a well-meaning, earnest Mormon. In Mormonism, the primary purpose of the gospel of Christ is to enable one to get back home to live again with Father God.[13] For Mormons, exalted salvation is understood as returning back home to their Father God. They return back to their premortal home of existence. Only in the highest Celestial heaven do God the Father and Jesus Christ dwell in fullness.

Although salvation in the highest Celestial heaven is what Mormons strive throughout their lives to achieve, the LDS Church is clear that many Latter-day Saints will never actually experience exalted salvation.[14] According to Mormonism, only a rather small remnant of worthy Mormons will actually experience eternal salvation—salvation in fullest glory—and return to live in the immediate presence of Father God.[15] These elect Mormons[16] who are deemed worthy and qualified through full obedience to enter the highest Celestial heaven are called the *Church of the Firstborn*. The Mormon members of the Church of the Firstborn are the Latter-day Saints who have kept all the Celestial laws and commandments.[17] These Mormons are the ones who remained fully worthy and obedient to the end of their mortal lives and even beyond death in the spirit-world's paradise.

The Church of the Firstborn consists only of Mormon men and women who have experienced an eternal Celestial marriage in the LDS temple and embrace the blessings of eternal progression and increase through giving birth to spirit-children.[18]

In the highest Celestial heaven, the LDS family has the opportunity to live forever as a family unit and can continue to grow as an eternal family.[19] Only in the highest Celestial heaven will Mormons be empowered to continue their eternal progression toward becoming gods. Mormonism also teaches that infant children—including the mentally impaired—who die before the age of individual accountability of eight years old will also be raised by their exalted parents.[20]

Partial Salvation

Mormonism teaches that any person failing to merit the fullest reward of exaltation in the highest level of the Celestial heaven will experience only a partial or incomplete salvation outside of the immediate presence of Father God in one of Mormonism's lesser degrees of eternal glory in the lower Celestial, Terrestrial, or Telestial kingdom.

The Three Heavenly Kingdoms of Mormonism

One must ask, "How did Mormonism come up with the belief that there are three heavens instead of just one heaven, as taught in Christianity?"[21] We find the answer in Joseph Smith's 1832 revelation that Mormons today call "the Vision of the Glories" or simply "the Vision." The rather perplexing details of the Vision are presently recorded in section 76 of the *Doctrine and Covenants*. The Vision was one of several revelations by Smith that emphasized the doctrine of heavenly exaltation and out of which the totally new Mormon understanding of eternal salvation emerged.[22]

The Vision—supposedly unveiling a vision of the three heavenly kingdoms and eternal hell—occurred suddenly when Joseph Smith and Sidney Rigdon were actively revising the Bible and contemplating the meaning of John 5:28–29, "Do not marvel at this, for an hour is coming when all who are in the tombs will hear his voice and come out, those who have done good to the resurrection of life, and those who have done evil to the resurrection of judgment."

Joseph Smith describes the situational context behind the Vision in the preface of *Doctrine and Covenants* 76:

Upon my return from Amherst conference, I resumed the translation of the Scriptures. From sundry revelations which had been received, it was apparent that many important points touching the salvation of man had been taken from the Bible, or lost before it was compiled. It appeared self-evident from what truths were left, that if God rewarded every one according to the deeds done in the body, the term "Heaven," as intended for the Saints' eternal home, must include more kingdoms than one. Accordingly, while translating St. John's Gospel, myself and Elder Rigdon saw the following vision.[23]

Complicating things even further, Latter-day Saints also claim that there are numerous internal hierarchical dwelling places within each of Smith's three heavens.[24] Dr. Stephen Robinson describes each of these three heavens as being very internally expansive and broad, and attempts to support his position by quoting Jesus' statement found in John 14:2, "In my Father's house are many rooms. If it were not so, would I have told you that I go to prepare a place for you?" As a result of this odd interpretation, Mormons teach that inside each of the three heavenly kingdoms are many degrees of glory to which every person will be permanently assigned following God's final judgment based on his or her behavior in mortality. Dr. Stephen Robinson writes:

After the resurrection of both the righteous and the wicked all human beings will be consigned to their final and permanent fate. From that verdict there will be no appeal or hope of release.[25]

Latter-day Saints believe that each person's eternal destiny will match what he or she has merited through good or bad works; the person will be rewarded or condemned according to what God determines he or she deserves.[26]

Smith's Revision and Reinterpretation of 1 Corinthians 15:35–49

In order to support his three-heaven theory in the afterlife, Joseph Smith revised and reinterpreted 1 Corinthians 15:40. In the Bible this verse reads:

> There are heavenly [celestial] bodies and earthly [terrestrial] bodies, but the glory of the heavenly is of one kind, and the glory of the earthly is of another.

But this is how it reads in the *Joseph Smith Translation*:

> Also celestial bodies, and bodies terrestrial, and bodies telestial; but the glory of the celestial, one; and the terrestrial, another; and the telestial, another.

As can be plainly seen, Joseph Smith rewrote the Bible. A basic reading of the biblical context of 1 Corinthians 15:35–49 shows that the apostle Paul is contrasting earthly and heavenly bodies in this Bible passage and not eternal distinct heavenly kingdoms as taught by Mormonism today.

The Lower Celestial Kingdom

As stated earlier, the LDS Church teaches that the Celestial kingdom has higher and lower levels.[27] The highest level of the Celestial kingdom is the fullness of heaven, but those who inhabit the lower Celestial level will experience only a partial or lesser salvation. This is important to understand because Mormon writings often simply speak about the Celestial kingdom without distinguishing between the higher and lower levels existing within it, which can lead to significant confusion.

The eternal residents of the lower Celestial level will consist of single Mormons who lived a worthy life of obedience, yet are disqualified from the highest Celestial heaven because they were never married in the temple.[28] Along with worthy single Mormons, good people—including Christians—who did not have an appropriate opportunity to hear and accept Mormonism on earth but would have received it if they had a chance, and accept the Mormon gospel in spirit-prison, will also dwell in the lower Celestial level.[29]

But these residents in the lower Celestial kingdom will be eternally separated from the immediate presence of God the Father and dwell separated from their families forever. They will be "damned," meaning that their progress toward godhood will end, and they will never experience increase by birthing spirit-children.[30] They will also be disqualified from becoming gods, instead having to settle for becoming angelic servants to the exalted Mormons dwelling in the highest Celestial heaven.

The Terrestrial Kingdom

Everyone assigned to the Terrestrial heaven will experience even a lesser degree and condition of glory than those in the lower Celestial level, as detailed in Joseph Smith's vision description recorded in *Doctrine and Covenants* 76:71–80, 91, 97.

The eternal residents of the Terrestrial heavenly kingdom will consist of unworthy or unfaithful Mormons. Although these Mormons accepted the LDS plan of salvation in their mortal lives, they were not sufficiently "valiant" in obeying all the principles and ordinances of the LDS gospel.[31] These Latter-day Saints were inactive, lukewarm, and nominal; they are often called *Jack Mormons*. Along with unworthy Mormons, the Terrestrial degree of glory will also be inhabited by good and honorable men and women who understood and intentionally rejected the so-called restored Mormon gospel on earth, but eventually accept it in spirit-prison after they die.[32]

These eternal residents in the Terrestrial kingdom will suffer forever and be filled with regret and misery, knowing that they could have earned a greater reward in glory. They will be tormented by the knowledge that they fell short of the requirements for Mormon exalted salvation, but in the end were just not good enough.[33] They will be eternally plagued with the consciousness that they just never measured up.

They will also be eternally separated from the direct presence of Father God, although Jesus will make periodic appearances. And they will live forever, separated from their family members, and have no opportunity to progress into godhood and birth spirit-children.

The Telestial Kingdom

As described by Joseph Smith in *Doctrine and Covenants* 76:81–90, 98–112, the Telestial kingdom is located at the bottom rung of the spiritual ladder of glory in Mormonism's three heavenly kingdoms, and is compared merely to the brightness of the moon. Mormonism emphasizes that the great majority of those who inhabited and suffered in spirit-prison will eventually enter the Telestial kingdom.[34]

The eternal residents of the Telestial kingdom will consist of extremely wicked people—adulterers, liars, thieves—who rejected the restored Mormon gospel in spirit-prison. They experience suffering and pain in paying for their sins. Those dwelling in the Telestial kingdom will be eternally separated from the presence of God the Father and Jesus, but will experience the presence of the Holy Spirit and angels.

Eternal Hell

The eternal hell of Mormonism—the second death, outer darkness, and the lake of fire and brimstone[35]—will be the condition and place of ultimate exile for Satan, demons, and what the Mormons call the *sons of perdition*. Joseph Smith's vision description of eternal hell is found in *Doctrine and Covenants* 76:25–49.

The eternal residents of hell will consist of Satan (Lucifer) and the millions of demons who are the spirit-children that sided with Lucifer in the preexistence rebellion against Father God. Satan and demons were cast out of heaven without potential of receiving bodies and so were excluded from progressing into gods. Their final destiny in eternal hell has been sealed since their preexistence rebellion.

Permanently consigned to eternal hell along with Satan and demons will be the extremely wicked and rebellious who rejected the Mormon gospel in spirit-prison, and also the sons of perdition or Mormon apostates who once accepted the so-called restored Mormon gospel with full revelation, but later rejected it and fell away. This is how Dr. Robert Millet defines *sons of perdition*:

> A son of perdition is one who commits the "unpardonable sin," the sin that will not be forgiven in this world or the world to come. One guilty of such an offense has enjoyed major revelation from God and yet has come out in open rebellion and opposition to the faith and thereby "sinned against the Holy Spirit." They inherit hereafter the kingdom of no glory.[36]

Mormon apostates—those who turn away from the supposed LDS restored gospel and leave the Mormon Church—even if they join a Christian church and are faithful followers of Jesus Christ—will be condemned and will suffer in eternal darkness and torment of hell forever.[37]

A Christian Perspective

Although there is a diversity of perspectives concerning the details of heaven and hell, the Christian position of Dr. Craig Blomberg is very persuasive:

> The biblical texts that speak of the different experiences we will all have before God on the judgment day (such as 1 Cor. 3:10–15) never suggest that such differences are perpetuated for all eternity. On the other hand, the idea of degrees of punishment in hell does fit biblical teaching (Luke 12:47–48), and it makes sense logically. After all, the lost will be judged on the basis of works, not by grace, and unsaved people vary greatly in the amount of evil they perpetrate.[38]

jesus, plus much more

This chapter will explain the teaching and practices of LDS salvation by examining and clarifying the meaning of Mormonism's third and fourth Articles of Faith creedal statements: "We believe that through the Atonement of Christ, all mankind may be saved,[1] by obedience to the laws and ordinances of the Gospel"[2] and "We believe that the first principles and ordinances of the Gospel are: first, Faith in the Lord Jesus Christ; second, Repentance; third, Baptism by immersion for the remission of sins; fourth, Laying on of hands for the gift of the Holy Ghost."

The Two-Way Covenant Salvation of Mormonism

It is very important to be aware that Mormonism's theology of salvation is understood as a two-way covenant made between God and man. In this sense, LDS salvation is a salvation partnership. Latter-day Saints state that God has fulfilled his part especially through the covenant grace in the atonement of Jesus Christ, and that humans must now fulfill their part by fully obeying the LDS covenant works and ordinances.[3]

In the LDS covenant plan of salvation, both God's grace and human works are absolutely necessary and required. In other words, although faith in God's covenant grace in the atonement of Jesus Christ is a prerequisite, the LDS Church also emphasizes very strongly that human covenant works and ordinances are also absolutely necessary for salvation. The LDS Church defines *ordinances* this way:

> In the Church, an ordinance is a sacred, formal act performed by the authority of the priesthood. Some ordinances are essential to our exaltation. These ordinances are called saving ordinances. They include baptism, confirmation, ordination to the Melchizedek Priesthood (for men), the temple endowment, and the marriage sealing. With each of these ordinances, we enter into solemn covenants with the Lord.[4]

This is why Dr. Robert Millet in his book *Grace Works* answers the question "Do Latter-day Saints believe in salvation by grace alone?" by saying, paradoxically, yes and no![5]

LDS Human Covenant Works

In Mormonism, the LDS requirement to experience eternal exaltation into godhood is best described as *Jesus, plus much more*.[6] As we will see in this chapter, Mormonism requires much more than faith in Jesus Christ to receive and experience the biblical promises of eternal life and salvation,[7] even though John 3:16 declares, "For God so loved the world, that he gave his only Son, that whoever believes in him should not perish but have eternal life," and the apostle Paul writes in Romans 6:23, "For the wages of sin is death, but the free gift of God is eternal life in Christ Jesus our Lord."

According to the LDS two-way covenant of salvation, putting one's total faith and trust in Jesus Christ's atonement is not sufficient to experience eternal life and exaltation with Father God in the afterlife.[8] If there is any question that Mormonism requires much more than Jesus Christ to receive and experience eternal life and exalted salvation, then the LDS *Book of Mormon Student Manual* settles the issue:

> One of the most fallacious doctrines originated by Satan and propounded by man is that man is saved alone by the grace of God; that belief in Jesus Christ alone is all that is needed for salvation.[9]

Bruce McConkie goes even further:

> One of the untrue doctrines found in modern Christendom is the concept that man can gain salvation—meaning in the kingdom of God—by grace alone and without obedience. This soul-destroying doctrine has the obvious effect of lessening the determination of an individual to conform to all of the laws and ordinances of the Gospel, such conformity being essential if the sought for reward is in reality to be gained.[10]

Mormons require numerous mandatory works of obedience in order to gain eternal life with God, and they have added several layers of LDS laws, conditions, and ordinances to the forgiving grace and redemptive power of Jesus Christ.

Latter-day Saints must accomplish and fulfill many things before the forgiveness and grace of Jesus is fully activated and effective in their lives.[11] This is what the third LDS Articles of Faith statement means when it states that eternal life requires human "obedience to the laws and ordinances of the Gospel." Dr. Stephen Robinson provides commentary on this creed:

> While there are no preconditions for entering into the covenant
> of faith in Christ to be justified by his grace through faith, there
> are covenant obligations incurred by so entering.[12]

According to LDS teaching, the highest level of eternal reward
and happiness is reserved only for those who entirely obey the
so-called restored LDS covenant obligations. In order for Latter-day Saints to enter the highest Celestial heaven, they must
place their trust in Jesus Christ and fully obey the Celestial
law, which consists of all the covenant obligations and works.
It is important to understand that Mormonism teaches that
the acceptance of the LDS version of the fullness of the gospel,
including faithfulness to all the LDS ordinances, is absolutely
necessary for salvation.[13]

The LDS requirement of faith in Jesus plus worthy Celestial
obedience to inherit eternal life is a heavy burden for many
Mormons. No matter how hard one tries to remain perfectly
obedient and keep all the extrabiblical Mormon commandments, falling short is inevitable. In living with the resultant
deep feelings of guilt and failure, many Mormons simply determine that they will never be good enough for Celestial
exaltation into gods, and they internally give up and become
resigned to the fact that they will be worthy of only a partial
or lesser salvation contained in the lower Mormon kingdoms.
Dr. Stephen Robinson presents numerous examples of Latter-
day Saints who are struggling with trying to be good enough
for Celestial exaltation, including his wife, Janet, who openly
confessed, "I'm never going to be perfect, and I just can't pre-
tend anymore that I am."[14]

Biblical Justification and Sanctification

Many Latter-day Saints accuse Christians of "cheap grace" or
"easy-believism" by neglecting the close relationship of faith and

works in the Bible. The shallowness of this Mormon accusation is discovered in the fact that, first, the LDS Church wrongly defines the content of biblical works—adding many works-obligations that do not exist in the Bible—and second, Mormons confuse the theological truths of biblical justification and sanctification.

Again, Mormonism teaches that entrance into the exalted state of eternal life in the highest level of the Celestial kingdom of God is assured only through faith in Jesus Christ plus good works—that is, works as defined and required by the so-called restored LDS gospel. But these requirements of extrabiblical Celestial works are a distortion of the gospel message that the righteous will live by faith alone.[15] The apostle Paul makes this LDS distortion of biblical salvation clear in Romans 1:16–17:

> For I am not ashamed of the gospel, for it is the power of God for salvation to everyone who believes, to the Jew first and also to the Greek. For in it the righteousness of God is revealed from faith for faith, as it is written, "The righteous shall live by faith."

Contradicting the Romans passage, Bruce McConkie defines the central salvation doctrine of justification this way:

> As with all other doctrines of salvation, justification is available because of the atoning sacrifice of Christ, but it becomes operative in the life of an individual only on conditions of personal righteousness.[16]

In stark contrast to the Mormon view of justification, Dr. John Piper in his insightful and well-researched book *Counted Righteous in Christ* clarifies in detail that God justifies the ungodly through the imputation[17] of his righteousness totally apart from any works.[18] Our justification—being declared righteous before God—fully rests in our authentic heart-centered faith in God; it is impossible to attain it through good works, even partially. The apostle Paul clearly affirms this truth in Ephesians 2:8–10:

> For by grace you have been saved through faith. And this is not your own doing; it is the gift of God, not a result of works, so that no one may boast. For we are his workmanship, created in Christ Jesus for good works, which God prepared beforehand, that we should walk in them.

Absolutely no works can serve as the effective means or instrument to justify ungodly humanity before our perfectly holy God.[19] Our justification and eternal salvation is experienced by faith alone, apart from every human concoction of works-righteousness.[20] In other words, biblically identified good works are the fruit of being justified by God in Christ, but they are not the authorized means of uniting us to Christ and meriting us eternal life with God.[21]

One of the top Christian theologians today, Dr. Wayne Grudem, in his definition of the doctrines of justification and sanctification, summarizes and reveals the vast divide between the Christian and Mormon views of salvation:

> Justification is an instantaneous legal act of God in which he thinks of our sins as forgiven and Christ's righteousness as belonging to us, and declares us righteous in his sight. Sanctification is a progressive work of God and man that makes us more and more free from sin and like Christ in our actual lives.[22]

It is important that we understand that in God's gospel of biblical salvation, the doctrines of justification and sanctification remain biblically inseparable and interrelated, but they are also distinct stand-alone truths. Sanctification must never be collapsed into the foundational doctrine of justification.[23]

Let's be clear: when Christians emphasize eternal life and salvation through faith in Jesus' righteousness alone, we do not exclude the importance of biblical works, but we simply understand how biblical works uniquely relate to the distinct doctrines of justification and sanctification. Dr. Craig Blomberg provides this clarity:

> Virtually all Evangelicals believe "that the proper way to harmonize the teaching of Scripture on faith and works is that only God's grace, received by faith, brings us into right standing before God (justification), a new birth—the beginning of new life with Christ (regeneration), liberation from bondage to past sin and its eternally damning consequences (redemption), and a new relationship with God and others (reconciliation). At this moment of conversion, the time of our salvation, God's Spirit comes to live in us and begins a process of moral transformation, unique to each person, often frustratingly slow and filled with setbacks, but nevertheless one that inevitably leads to perseverance in good works of all different kinds, though never quantifiable and never adequate to merit eternal life with God in and of themselves."[24]

Because the various LDS salvation covenant requirements for Mormon eternal exaltation can be confusing, for clarification purposes they are organized in this chapter under three general categories: (1) the first principles and ordinances of the gospel, (2) salvation temple ordinances, and (3) remaining a worthy Mormon to the end.

The First Principles and Ordinances of the Gospel

Mormonism's fourth Articles of Faith creedal statement reads, "We believe that the first principles and ordinances of the Gospel are: first, Faith in the Lord Jesus Christ; second, Repentance;

third, Baptism by immersion for the remission of sins; fourth, Laying on of hands for the gift of the Holy Ghost."

Faith in Jesus Christ and Repentance

Although I firmly believe that the LDS gospel is a "distorted gospel," not a "restored gospel" (see Gal. 1:7), Mormonism does teach faith in Jesus Christ and personal repentance of our sins. This is how the LDS Church defines *repentance*:

> Repentance is one of the first principles of the gospel and is essential to our temporal and eternal happiness. It is much more than just acknowledging wrongdoings. It is a change of mind and heart that gives us a fresh view about God, about ourselves, and about the world. It includes turning away from sin and turning to God for forgiveness. It is motivated by love for God and the sincere desire to obey His commandments.[25]

Mormons do believe that humans will be punished for their sins if they do not respond to Jesus' atoning death[26] on the cross. In fact, each week during their church services they partake in communion of bread and water in remembrance and confession of Jesus Christ's atoning death.

The third LDS Articles of Faith creedal statement emphasizes that Mormons teach and believe in the atonement of Jesus Christ. This is how the official LDS Web site describes Jesus' atonement:

> As used in the scriptures, to atone is to suffer the penalty for sins, thereby removing the effects of sin from the repentant sinner and allowing him or her to be reconciled to God. Jesus Christ was the only one capable of carrying out the Atonement for all mankind. Because of His Atonement, all people will be resurrected, and those who obey His gospel will receive the gift of eternal life with God.[27]

Mormonism does not believe a person's sins are forgiven without the person's first putting his or her faith in the atonement of Jesus Christ. Let us emphasize once more: the LDS Church does distort and twist many biblical truths concerning eternal salvation, but it does confess and believe that Jesus—although falsely and heretically identified as a spirit-son of Father God—was incarnated in the flesh (see John 1:1–18; Phil. 2), lived a perfect and sinless life, died on the cross, was buried, was resurrected, and was and will always be the one and only messianic Savior of our world. In this general sense, Mormonism reflects the first truths of New Testament Christianity as presented by the apostle Paul, which he calls the first truths of the gospel:

> For I delivered to you as of first importance what I also received: that Christ died for our sins in accordance with the Scriptures, that he was buried, [and] that he was raised on the third day in accordance with the Scriptures (1 Cor. 15:3–4).

Faith in Jesus Christ's atonement on the cross and personal repentance is an essential component of Mormonism. The more recent LDS books by Brigham Young University professors such as Dr. Stephen Robinson and Robert Millet have focused on and articulated this component more clearly than has historical Mormonism. Unfortunately, however, Mormonism's requirement to put one's faith in Jesus Christ and repent is easily lost and made functionally dormant under a heavy load of extrabiblical salvation requirements and works foreign to all the main branches of Christianity.

It is important to emphasize that Mormonism's faith in Jesus Christ and repentance provides a person with only the *opportunity* to earn a position in one of the three LDS kingdoms through obedient covenant works, and does not *guarantee* eternal life with God. There is a significant difference between Jesus' simply providing us an *opportunity* to merit eternal life, and being the absolute and sufficient *guarantee* of eternal life as taught in Christianity.

Water Baptism and Joining the Mormon Church

Following faith in Jesus Christ and repentance, new Mormon converts are required to submit to the ordinance of water baptism[28] by immersion[29] for the remission or forgiveness of their sins, and as the means of becoming official members of the LDS Church.[30]

Mormonism teaches that water baptism must be performed by an ordained male in either the Aaronic or Melchizedek LDS priesthood. If a person is not baptized in the LDS Church, that person does not experience forgiveness or remission of his or her sins. It is important to keep in mind that Latter-day Saints reject the legitimacy of water baptisms performed at all Christian churches. All Christian water baptisms are deemed unacceptable, unauthorized, and invalid before God. Most Christians agree that water baptism is a vital act of obedience, but that simply failing to be baptized does not cause us to lose our salvation because eternal life is based on our faith in Jesus Christ alone. As a friend of mine often says, we believe in Jesus plus nothing.

The Mormon sacrament of water baptism is performed only once, and is available to anyone who has reached the age of eight, the age of personal accountability and under-standing in the LDS Church.[31] Water baptism is performed by the LDS priesthood in a large sunken pool or baptismal font—approximately four feet deep and six to ten feet in width and length—located in most Mormon church meeting houses. During the saving ordinance of water baptism, the authorized Mormon male facilitating the baptism must recite exactly pre-scribed words over the person being baptized. This is how the *Encyclopedia of Mormonism* describes the baptismal prayer:

When an individual is baptized, the person with the proper priesthood authority goes down into the water with the candidate, raises his right arm to the square, calls the individual by the full legal name, and says, "Having been commissioned of Jesus Christ, I baptize you in the name of the Father, and of the Son, and of the Holy Ghost. Amen," and then immerses the candidate.[32]

For clarification, water baptism ordinances performed within Mormon temples are not the same type of water baptism as the saving church sacrament performed in Mormon churches. Water baptisms performed in Mormon temples are proxy baptisms performed by individual Mormons for the salvation of the dead. This topic is explained in more detail in chapter 10.

Contrary to the Mormon requirement of a saving baptism performed by a member of the LDS priesthood, the Bible teaches in Romans 10:9–10 that we experience God's salvation if we confess with our mouth that Jesus is Lord and believe in our heart that God raised him from the dead. For with the heart one believes and is justified, and with the mouth one confesses and is saved. Water baptism is a symbolic outward demonstration of our inner heart's faith in Jesus Christ alone for salvation, and is accepted by God not based on the one who performs it, but on the authenticity of the faith of the one who experiences it.

Holy Ghost Confirmation

Mormons believe that immediately following water baptism, a person receives the "gift of the Holy Ghost" through the laying on of hands by the ordained male members of the LDS Melchizedek Priesthood. Mormons call this ordinance "Holy Ghost confirmation." Mormonism emphasizes that although people may occasionally and temporarily feel the presence of the Holy Spirit in their lives, not until they are officially confirmed by the authority of the LDS priesthood through the laying on of hands are they able to experience the constant indwelling companionship and advocacy of the Holy Spirit.[33]

But the idea that a person can receive the indwelling advocacy, ever-present assurance, and sustaining power of the Holy Spirit only through the ordained laying on of hands by the Mormon priesthood is foreign to the teaching of the Bible, as the apostle Paul indicates in Ephesians 1:13: "In him you also, when you heard the word of truth, the gospel of your salvation, and believed in him, were sealed with the promised Holy Spirit."

Salvation Temple Ordinances

Besides the saving ordinances of water baptism and Holy Spirit confirmation, Mormonism also requires individuals to experience detailed temple ordinances to earn eternal exaltation into gods. As one Mormon writer states, "The temple opens the gate to us to be equal with God."[34] This is how Mormons view their temples:

> Temples are literally houses of the Lord. They are holy places of worship where individuals make sacred covenants with God. Because making covenants with God is such a solemn responsibility, individuals cannot enter the temple to receive their endowments or be sealed in marriage for eternity until they have fully prepared themselves and been members of the Church for at least a year. Throughout history, the Lord has commanded His people to build temples. The Church is working to build temples all over the world to make temple blessings more available for a greater number of Heavenly Father's children.[35]

Through the temple ordinances, a Mormon takes one huge step forward in obtaining entrance into the highest level of the Celestial heaven. At strong odds with Christianity, LDS temple ordinances have no support in the Bible. These LDS temple ordinances are totally based on and configured by modern Mormon revelations, and are an esoteric tradition that Mormons believe is an integral part of the restored gospel of the Latter-day Saints.[36]

No Temples in New Testament Christianity

Before we explore the saving ordinances of the Mormon temple, it is important to clarify that the Christian church has never constructed exclusive and private temples for secret rituals, sacraments, or worship.[37] In fact, the Bible is clear that Christian people—the body of Christ—are now God's true temple under the covenant of Jesus Christ in the New Testament. Under the new covenant, the Holy Spirit dwells in God's people, and not in special physical temple buildings made with human hands. The apostle Paul makes this obvious: "Do you not know that you are God's temple and that God's Spirit dwells in you?" (1 Cor. 3:16); "For we are the temple of the living God" (2 Cor. 6:16). It is very far-fetched and completely unwarranted for Mormons to suggest that temples were used by the New Testament church, and that they needed to be restored back to the earth.

Jesus emphatically stated in John 4:21–23 that his true new-covenant followers will worship God in spirit and truth, and no longer need temples as seen in the Old Testament:

> Jesus said to her, "Woman, believe me, the hour is coming when neither on this mountain nor in Jerusalem will you worship the Father. You worship what you do not know; we worship what we know, for salvation is from the Jews. But the hour is coming, and is now here, when the true worshipers will wor-

ship the Father in spirit and truth, for the Father is seeking such people to worship him."

Jesus' words came to pass during his crucifixion when the temple veil was ripped from top to bottom (see Matt. 27:50–51), signifying that there is now free access to God through the blood of Christ and that Christ alone is our High Priest and only Mediator before God. Physical temples are irrelevant and unnecessary for holy Christian living, and are totally foreign to all New Testament teaching. This is how the writer of Hebrews 10:19–21 says it:

> Therefore, brothers, . . . we have confidence to enter the holy places by the blood of Jesus, by the new and living way that he opened for us through the curtain, that is, through his flesh, and . . . we have a great priest over the house of God.

If this is the case, then where did Mormons get the idea of building and using temples for sacred and secretive rituals not found in the Bible? Although Joseph Smith adopted the use of a temple from the Old Testament, there is solid evidence that he borrowed the practice of using secret rituals from the Masons or Freemasons. We know that Joseph Smith became a practicing Mason in March 1842, and quickly progressed to the high position of Master Mason. The Masons considered their lodges to be temples, and many of their secret rituals, signs, and symbols are reflected in the temple practices of Mormonism today.[38]

Becoming a Temple-Worthy Mormon

Before a Mormon can complete the ordinances and rituals conducted inside the temple that are required for exaltation to a god, the person first must be a Mormon member for one year and receive certified and authorized permission to have regular access inside. Although it is generally known that a non-Mormon can enter an LDS temple only during specially designated times,[39] it is a significant surprise to those outside the LDS Church when they discover that Mormons themselves cannot enter the temple without official annual examination and authorization.

Before a Mormon can enter the temple to experience and perform its sacred and secret ordinances, he or she must first be examined and be authorized a "temple-worthy" Mormon by an LDS ward bishop. This temple interview contains a prescribed set of probing questions into the lifestyle and beliefs of a Mormon to verify that the person has good standing within the LDS Church and is qualified or worthy to enter the sacred temple. The deeply personal and inquiring obedience questions asked of Mormons relate to moral cleanliness and purity, living by the Word of Wisdom revelation,[40] ensuring that they are paying their tithes in full, confessing basic LDS doctrine, and several others.

A Card-Carrying Mormon

Once interviewed by an LDS bishop and determined to be in good standing and worthy, the Mormon is then issued a "temple recommend" identification card about the dimensions of a wallet-sized driver's license that authorizes the person to go in and out of the temple for one year only. A temple-worthy Mormon must be interviewed by a ward bishop annually in order to ensure that he or she has remained a faithful and worthy LDS member.

Card-carrying Mormons show their signed authorization at the recommend desk located in an area just inside the temple door. Mormons will show their recommend cards each time they enter the temple. In fact, Mormonism has now added a bar code to their recommend cards so that they simply need to be swiped for approval.

Since the temple ordinances are absolute requirements for Mormons to eventually enter eternal exaltation, to be denied access to the Mormon temple generally assures that they will experience only a partial or incomplete salvation after they die. They will be found worthy to enter only a lower level of the heavenly kingdom outside of the presence of God the Father.

The Internal Design of Mormon Temples

For Mormons, their temples are considered the most sacred structures on earth, and are carefully and strategically designed with certain floors, sections, and rooms to accommodate LDS ordinances and ceremonies.[41] Most of the LDS temple interiors are similar to those of luxury hotels.

The ground floor of a Mormon temple has administration office spaces and locker rooms where temple-worthy Mormons change into all-white clothing to perform various sacraments. Men wear white shirts and pants, and women wear long white dresses. Although Mormons can rent their temple clothes, many bring their own.

The lower floor is where the large baptistries—surrounded by twelve carved oxen representing the tribes of Israel—are located. Mormons are baptized for the dead in these ornate baptistries.

The most sacred rooms within the temple, however, are located on the upper floor, where one finds the "ordinance rooms" for endowments and the "sealing rooms" for Celestial marriages and family sealings. The top floor also contains the one and only "Celestial Room," which symbolizes the highest level of the Celestial heaven. The Celestial Room represents the holy of holies in the LDS temple.

The Sacred and Secretive Temple Ordinances

All Mormon temples are closed on Sundays as the Latter-day Saints worship at their local church meetinghouses. In contrast to the "low church" simple worship services held weekly at Mormon meetinghouses, the LDS temple ordinances or sacraments are extremely ritualistic, ceremonial, and symbolic. Mormons consider these ordinances very sacred. Great secrecy accompanies these sacred temple rituals.[42] In fact, Mormons make a covenant not to discuss the details of the LDS temple or its ordinances to anyone else—inside or outside Mormonism.[43]

The two types of secret ordinances and rituals practiced in the Mormon temples are those for the living (described below) and those done by proxy for the dead. The temple ordinances performed for the dead will be explored in the next chapter.

The Temple Washing and Anointing

A Mormon who enters the LDS temple for the first time is called a *patron*. The initial ordinance that a patron is required to participate in is called *washing and anointing*. The patron enters the men's or women's locker room, where he or she exchanges street clothes for a poncho-like robe that is slipped on over the head and that is open on both sides. Mormons call this their "shield." Wearing the shield over his or her naked body, the patron enters the men's or women's washing and anointing room. Here an authorized temple worker ceremonially washes and blesses the individual's body. Following this body washing, the patron is then anointed with olive oil. After each washing and anointing, two temple workers lay their hands on the patron's head and confirm him or her.

After this ritual washing and anointing, the patron is taken to a curtained room where the temple worker takes off the shield and puts temple garments on the patron. Sewn into the temple garments are markings, similar to those used in Freemasonry, resembling a backward *L* over the right breast and a capital *V* over the left breast. When the temple garments are placed on the new temple patron, the person is given a new sacred name that is never to be told to anyone.

The Temple Endowment

The temple endowment is a totally extrabiblical ritual institutionalized by Joseph Smith in 1842 only a few months after becoming a Freemason. The temple endowment is considered to be a very sacred spiritual blessing given only to worthy and faithful LDS members. It is an in-depth and complex experience that prepares Mormons to return someday to the presence of Father God in the highest Celestial heaven. Mormons receiving this ordinance receive secret information that will be relevant to their lives in the Celestial world. They are also given special handshakes called *tokens* and secret signs and words during the endowment ordinance. Richard and Joan Ostling's well-researched book *Mormon America* provides a concise description of the endowment ordinance:

> The endowment ceremony, today, as described publicly by the church, has four main segments: (1) a drama, formerly by live actors but since the 1950s presented on film, which presents the story of salvation and redemption as a human journey moving from pre-earthly beginnings, through the Creation and Fall, and Christ's life and death (2) progression to a brighter room, where believers learn about God's blessings (3) an exchange of promises from God, then moving through an opening in a curtain or veil to represent the passage from this life into immortality (4) and entrance into the Celestial Room, representing the highest level of heaven.[44]

When Mormons experience their endowment ritual, they wear special ceremonial clothing and sacred white underclothing called *temple garments*.[45] Before they leave the temple, they take off the ceremonial outer clothes, but continue to wear the undergarments beneath their normal clothes. Mormons make a covenant to wear these undergarments for the rest of their lives, at all times. Wearing these special undergarments day and night is to remind them of the sacred covenants that they have made in the temple.

The Temple Celestial Marriages of Exaltation

An individual's hope of becoming a god in the highest Celestial heaven of glory can be achieved only through participating in an eternal marriage ceremony inside a Mormon temple. As a result, Celestial temple marriage is the most important requirement in Mormonism's Celestial salvation plan.

Marriage partners sealed in a temple ceremony will be together forever and will have a family of spirit-children. Any Mormon who is not married in the temple or remains single will not return to Father God in the highest Celestial heaven. In Mormonism, eternal salvation in the highest Celestial kingdom is a family affair.[46] So the familiar LDS saying "Families Are Forever" is much more than a public-relations slogan; it is deeply rooted in Mormonism's theology of being exalted into godhood. Those eternally married in the temple can apply to have their Celestial marriage unsealed—meaning a Mormon divorce—by the authority of the Mormon priesthood.[47]

The Temple Family Sealings

Mormonism declares that children who are born to a couple married in the temple are automatically "sealed" to their parents for eternity. Parents who had their children before their Celestial temple marriage must have their families "sealed" to them in a separate ceremony performed in a special family sealing room in the temple.[48]

Mormons who believe their eternal temple marriages and family sealings will automatically guarantee that their families will dwell together in the Celestial kingdom are badly misguided. Although marriage and family sealings are prerequisites for Celestial salvation, each Mormon family member will enter only the eternal kingdom level that he or she merits. So if a spouse or child, even if sealed in the temple, is not found worthy to enter the highest level in the Celestial kingdom, then that person will be eternally separated from his or her family unit. In other words, personal worthiness, not temple sealing ordinances alone, is what determines whether families will be together for eternity.

Remaining a Worthy Mormon to the End

Mormons must remain worthy and obedient to the required LDS Celestial covenants and laws their entire lives to have any assurance of becoming gods in the highest Celestial kingdom. Individual Mormons must endure and remain fully worthy until the end, even beyond death in paradise.

How do Latter-day Saints remain worthy Mormons? Besides personal holiness and several other covenant obligations, two of the central requirements are that they obey the Law of Tithing and follow the requirements of Joseph Smith's Word of Wisdom revelation.

The Law of Tithing

The payment of a full tithe, usually understood as 10 percent of one's gross income by most Mormons, is expected of worthy Mormons and is necessary to progress into godhood. For Mormons, the Law of Tithing is the law of eternal inheritance.[49] Mormons can jeopardize their inheritance in the Celestial kingdom if he or she failed to tithe in full.

It is understood within the LDS Church that a person who obeys or disobeys the Law of Tithing reveals whether he or she is truly for the kingdom of God or against it.[50] Every year each Mormon has a "tithing settlement" meeting with the ward bishop to ensure that he or she has paid the full tithe. If not, the person will be admonished and the salvation consequences will be explained.[51] Although Mormons are not excommunicated for not tithing in full, they are excluded from holding major leadership roles and from having access to the temple ordinances.

Obeying the Word of Wisdom Revelation

Obedience to Joseph Smith's Word of Wisdom revelation recorded in *Doctrine and Covenants* section 89 is an essential requirement of Mormon worthiness.[52] To remain a worthy Mormon, the person must totally abstain from wine, alcoholic drinks, tobacco, coffee, and tea.

Reading the historical context that motivated Smith's Word of Wisdom revelation is very interesting, insightful, and even odd, especially since the LDS Church emphasizes that our position in eternity is dependent on this revelation's complete obedience. This is the history given by the official LDS student manual on *Doctrine and Covenants* section 89:

> The first school of the prophets was held in a small room situated over the Prophet Joseph's kitchen, in a house which belonged to Bishop Whitney. The brethren came to that place from hundreds of miles to attend school in a little room probably no larger than eleven by fourteen. When they assembled together in this room after breakfast, the first thing they did was to light their pipes and, while smoking, talk about the great things of the kingdom and spit all over the room, and as soon as the pipe was out of their mouths a large chew of tobacco would then be taken. Often when the Prophet entered the room to give the school instructions he would find himself in a cloud of tobacco smoke. This, and the complaints of his wife having to clean so filthy a floor, made the Prophet think upon the matter, and he inquired of the Lord relating to the conduct

of the Elders in using tobacco, and the revelation known as the Word of Wisdom was the result of his inquiry.[53]

Our human righteousness—no matter how heroic it might be—falls short of the glory of God. Biblical salvation is righteousness, peace, and joy in the Holy Spirit, based on the following truths: "For the wages of sin is death, but the free gift of God is eternal life in Christ Jesus our Lord" (Rom. 6:23); "For by grace you have been saved through faith. And this is not your own doing; it is the gift of God, not a result of works, so that no one may boast" (Eph. 2:8–9).

In celebration of the saving gift of eternal life in Jesus Christ, this chapter concludes with the apostle Paul's declaration found in Romans 8:31–39, for it seems to sum everything up:

> What then shall we say to these things? If God is for us, who can be against us? He who did not spare his own Son but gave him up for us all, how will he not also with him graciously give us all things? Who shall bring any charge against God's elect? It is God who justifies. Who is to condemn? Christ Jesus is the one who died—more than that, who was raised—who is at the right hand of God, who indeed is interceding for us. Who shall separate us from the love of Christ? Shall tribulation, or distress, or persecution, or famine, or nakedness, or danger, or sword? As it is written, "For your sake we are being killed all the day long; we are regarded as sheep to be slaughtered." No, in all these things we are more than conquerors through him who loved us. For I am sure that neither death nor life, nor angels nor rulers, nor things present nor things to come, nor powers, nor height nor depth, nor anything else in all creation, will be able to separate us from the love of God in Christ Jesus our Lord.

HOW THE DEAD ARE SAVED IN MORMONISM

What happens after we die? This is a very relevant question that most people think about and seek answers for. Based on Hebrews 9:27 ("it is appointed for man to die once, and after that comes judgment"), Christianity in general believes that humankind's final eternal destiny is determined and permanent immediately upon physical death.[1]

This chapter explains how Mormonism, in contrast to Christianity, has developed an elaborate teaching concerning an after-death spirit-world, a corresponding salvation scheme for the dead,[2] and why Joseph Smith declared to the Latter-day Saints that "the greatest responsibility in this world that God has laid upon us is to seek after our dead."[3]

Elijah and the Mormon Salvation for the Dead

Christians are aware of the ministry story of the Old Testament prophet Elijah, but may be surprised to discover that Elijah played a major role in Mormonism's doctrine of salvation for the dead as emphasized in *Doctrine and Covenants* section 2.[4] Mormonism oddly asserts that the latter-day ministry of Elijah to authorize Mormons to perform the salvation temple ordinances for the dead is referred to in Malachi 4:5–6: "Behold, I will send you Elijah the prophet before the great and awesome day of the LORD comes. And he will turn the hearts of fathers to their children and the hearts of children to their fathers."[5]

Mormons emphasize that Elijah appeared to Peter and John with Jesus on the Mount of Transfiguration,[6] at which time Jesus is said to have given them the divine ruling keys, authority, and power of the kingdom of God on earth. On September 21, 1823, the angel Moroni apparently told Joseph Smith that the Lord would give him the priesthood authority through Elijah in fulfillment of Malachi 4:5–6.

In Mormon thinking, Moroni's declaration was fulfilled on April 3, 1836, when Elijah supposedly visited Joseph Smith and Oliver Cowdery in the Kirtland temple, and ordained them with the sealing authority and power of the kingdom of God to bind on earth and in heaven.[7] According to Mormons, this visitation of Elijah in the Kirtland temple inaugurated the latter-day Mormon salvation that could extend to both the living and the dead.

Appealing to Jesus' words in Matthew 18:18, "Truly, I say to you, whatever you bind on earth shall be bound in heaven, and whatever you loose on earth shall be loosed in heaven," Mormons believe that God has given the LDS male priesthood the salvation power and authority to bind on earth and seal eternally in heaven. In other words, Mormonism believes that the latter-day spirit of Elijah is the Mormon priesthoods' divine ability to redeem the dead, which enables them to bind in heaven all LDS covenants, obligations, vows, and ordinances made on earth.[8] Latter-day Saints are told that all the covenants and ordinances performed on earth that are not directly sealed by the LDS priesthood are temporal and end when someone dies.[9]

The Mormon Spirit-World

Mormons teach that after people die, they will go to dwell in a place identified as the spirit-world. The spirit-world is a temporary home for all disembodied human spirits where they will exist between their death and future resurrection. Many Latter-day Saints apparently believe that the spirit-world is located right here on earth. They emphasize that a very thin veil exists between the living and the dead, and that their dead family members are near them at all times.

Based on the *Book of Mormon*'s Alma 40:11, the general Mormon understanding of the spirit-world was initially revealed by an angel. It reads: "Concerning the state of the soul between death and the resurrection—Behold, it has been made known unto me by an angel."[10] But Mormonism's detailed salvation scheme for the dead is primarily based on the modern revelations found in *Doctrine and Covenants* sections 2, 127, 128, and 138 and Enrichment O, and not in the Bible.[11]

According to Mormonism, after people die they are sent by God to one of two places—either paradise or spirit-prison—in this intermediate spirit-world. Worthy Mormons will enter paradise, but everyone else—including unfaithful Mormons, Christians, and the rest of humanity—will be sent to spirit-prison to atone for their sins. Mormon theology teaches that everyone in the spirit-world will live and function exactly as they did while living on earth, possessing the same beliefs, attitudes, and talents.[12]

Mormon Paradise

After they die, all faithful and worthy Mormons will enter a glorious dwelling place in the spirit-world called *paradise*.[13] This understanding is supported by the following statement found in the LDS official manual *True to the Faith*:

> Paradise designates a place of peace and happiness in the post-mortal spirit world, reserved for those who have been baptized and who have remained faithful.[14]

The *Book of Mormon's* Alma 40:12 describes paradise in the spirit-world as a wonderful place of happiness and peace:

> The spirits of those who are righteous are received into a state of happiness, which is called paradise, a state of rest, a state of peace, where they shall rest from all their troubles and from all care, and sorrow.

While living in paradise, faithful Latter-day Saints will continue to grow and prepare for their final destiny in either the Celestial or Terrestrial kingdom after their resurrection, depending on their personal worthiness.

Spirit-Prison

Unfaithful Mormons, Christians, and the rest of humanity will be sent to spirit-prison—also known as *hell* or *outer darkness* by Latter-day Saints—in the spirit-world.[15] Those in spirit-prison will have an opportunity to pay for their sins, learn the gospel of Jesus Christ, and receive LDS temple ordinances.[16]

Spirit-prison is a condition and place of self-determined spiritual imprisonment and torment. This is the description of spirit-prison found in the *Book of Mormon's* Alma 40:13–14:

And then shall it come to pass, that the spirits of the wicked, yea, who are evil—for behold, they have no part nor portion of the Spirit of the Lord; for behold, they chose evil works rather than good; therefore the spirit of the devil did enter into them, and take possession of their house—and these shall be cast out into outer darkness; there shall be weeping, and wailing, and gnashing of teeth, and this because of their own iniquity, being led captive by the will of the devil. Now this is the state of the souls of the wicked, yea, in darkness, and a state of awful, fearful looking for the fiery indignation of the wrath of God upon them; thus they remain in this state, as well as the righteous in paradise, until the time of their resurrection.

Those dwelling in spirit-prison will suffer a spiritual death of tormenting hell,[17] and will experience nonstop weeping, wailing, and gnashing of teeth under the wrath and judgment of God. This is how Bruce McConkie describes the terrible experience of spirit-prison:

That part of the spirit world inhabited by wicked spirits who are awaiting the eventual day of their resurrection is called hell. Between their death and resurrection, these souls of the wicked are cast out into outer darkness, into the gloomy depression of sheol, into the hades of waiting wicked spirits, into hell. There they suffer torments of the damned; there they welter in the vengeance of eternal fire; there is found weeping and wailing and gnashing of teeth; there the fiery indignation of the wrath of God is poured out upon the wicked.[18]

Spirit-prison is a very dark place of deep depression and awful fear where people will suffer torment and pay for their earthly sins as they wait for the final judgment of God.[19] Following the resurrection and God's final judgment at the end of the millennium, those still dwelling in spirit-prison will either go to the Telestial kingdom or be condemned to eternal hell, which is explained in more detail at the end of this chapter.

Jesus' Ministry in Paradise

Mormons teach that during the three days between Jesus' burial and resurrection, he visited the spirit-world and ministered to the righteous Latter-day Saints dwelling in paradise. Dr. Robert Millet writes:

> Between the time of Christ's death on the cross and his rise from the tomb, he went into the postmortal spirit world, preached his gospel, organized the faithful, in order that the message of truth might be made available to all who are willing to receive it.[20]

Mormons base their teaching on this Bible passage:

> For Christ also suffered once for sins, the righteous for the unrighteous, that he might bring us to God, being put to death in the flesh but made alive in the spirit, in which he went and proclaimed to the spirits in prison, because they formerly did not obey, when God's patience waited in the days of Noah, while the ark was being prepared, in which a few, that is, eight persons, were brought safely through water (1 Peter 3:18–20).

This passage has had many interpretations, but perhaps the best one is presented by Dr. Craig Blomberg, rejecting the suggestion that Jesus offered salvation to dead humans or spirits in prison:

> This passage describes Christ's announcement of victory over the demonic world (so directly involved in that particularly wicked era just prior to the flood, 2 Peter 2:4) than any postmortem offer of repentance to the unevangelized.

According to LDS teaching, before Jesus' ministry in paradise, those suffering God's wrath in spirit-prison were unable to repent, accept the LDS plan of salvation, and cross over into the realm of Mormon paradise.[21] After Jesus' ministry in paradise, however, those dwelling in spirit-prison are now given an opportunity to repent, accept the LDS plan of salvation and ordinances, and enter Mormon paradise.

Paradise's Mormon Missionaries

Latter-day Saints believe that when Jesus supposedly visited paradise during his three days in the grave, he commissioned paradise Mormons to become missionaries to those suffering in spirit-prison.[22] The *Encyclopedia of Mormonism* explains Jesus' visit this way:

> He organized the righteous forces and appointed messengers, clothed with power and authority, and commissioned them to go forth and carry the light of the gospel to them that were in darkness (prison-hell).[23]

This missionary work in spirit-prison by paradise Mormons is what the Latter-day Saints say is meant by 1 Peter 4:6: "For this is why the gospel was preached even to those who are dead, that though judged in the flesh the way people are, they might live in the spirit the way God does." In fact, Mormonism believes that the most magnificent and extensive missionary program is taking place in the spirit-world right now, as President Brigham Young concludes:

> Compare those inhabitants on the earth who have heard the Gospel in our day, with the millions who have never heard it, or had the keys of salvation presented to them, and you will conclude at once as I do, that there is an almighty work to perform in the spirit world.[24]

Mormon Salvation in Spirit-Prison

As stated above, the Latter-day Saints teach an elaborate salvation scheme that provides a second chance for those dwelling in spirit-prison to convert and become faithful Mormons. Joseph Smith emphasized that it is "no more incredible that God should save the dead, than that he should raise the dead."[25] This is a very central and complex doctrine in Mormonism. This LDS teaching is presented in very broad generalities, however, and many specifics are often lacking and not clarified.

Becoming a Mormon in Spirit-Prison

According to Mormonism, if the spirits dwelling in spirit-prison respond to the preaching of the Mormon missionaries, repent, and put their faith in the salvation plan of the Latter-day Saints, they will have an opportunity to leave spirit-prison and join the righteous Mormons living in beautiful paradise.[26] But this permanent move from spirit-prison to paradise is not automatic. Under the LDS doctrine of salvation for the dead, the spirits that convert to Mormonism in spirit-prison can transfer to paradise only after worthy Mormons on earth have performed required temple ordinances on their behalf and in their name.[27]

The Second-Chance Confusion of Mormonism

There seems to be some confusion, even among some Mormons, about what this second-chance salvation for the dead really means and actually entails, especially as it relates to entering the Celestial kingdom.[28]

In authoritative Mormon teaching, a person who properly understood and rejected Mormonism during his or her earthly life will never have a second opportunity to enter the Celestial kingdom, even if the person repents of his or her sins and receives all the required proxy temple ordinances. Bruce McConkie is precise on this doctrinal fact:

> There is no such thing as a second chance to gain salvation by accepting the gospel in the spirit world after spurning, declining, or refusing to accept it in this life. It is true that there may be

a second chance to hear and accept the gospel, but those who have thus procrastinated their acceptance of the saving truths will not gain salvation in the celestial kingdom of God.[29]

Salvation for the dead is limited expressly to those who do not have opportunity in this life to accept the gospel but who would have taken the opportunity had it come to them.[30]

There is no promise in any revelation that those who have a fair and just opportunity in this life to accept the gospel, and who do not do it, will have another chance in the spirit world to gain celestial salvation.[31]

In other words, entrance into the Celestial salvation is available only to those in spirit-prison who have never had an opportunity during their mortal lives to hear and understand the LDS restored gospel, and based on the foreknowledge of God would have become Mormons if they had had the chance.[32] Dr. Stephen Robinson clarifies:

Persons who did not have the opportunity of baptism presented to them during their lives may still inherit the celestial kingdom if in the infinite foreknowledge of God they would have received it given the opportunity.[33]

In the LDS view it is only those who have heard the gospel fairly and correctly presented, who understand it correctly, who feel a witness of the Spirit and who yet refuse to accept it who will bring their spiritual progress to a halt.[34]

Thus, everyone, even family members of worthy Mormons, who understood, rejected, or were unfaithful to the LDS restored gospel during their earthly lives will have the opportunity to enter only the Terrestrial or Telestial kingdom following the final judgment of God. This means that, in the end, they will be eternally separated from their family members who go to the Celestial kingdom, whether temple family sealings were performed for them or not. Personal worthiness is the Mormon assurance or guarantee concerning whether family units will dwell together for eternity, and not temple family sealings.

Mormon Temple Work for the Dead

Latter-day Saints identify the performance of proxy temple ordinances—water baptism, endowments, and family sealings—as *temple work*. This is how Dr. Robert Millet describes LDS temple work:

> Because the sacraments or ordinances of the Church are earthly ordinances and must be performed on this side of the veil of death, Latter-day Saints go into temples to receive the sacraments in behalf of those who have died without them.[35]

The *Encyclopedia of Mormonism* explains the nature of the LDS temple ordinances for the dead this way:

> Temple ordinances are not mere signs. They are channels of the Spirit that enable one to be born of God in the fullest sense and to receive all the covenants and blessings of Jesus Christ. The performing of earthly ordinances by proxy for those who have died is as efficacious and vitalizing as if the deceased person had done them. That person, in turn, is free to accept or reject the ordinances in the spirit-world.[36]

The LDS Church makes it clear to its members that many Mormon converts and family members are continuing to abide in spirit-prison as they wait to receive proxy temple ordinances on their behalf. As a result, individual Mormons experience a tremendous amount of pressure by LDS Church officials to dedicate a significant amount of time and effort in performing their temple duties for the dead:

> Some of us have had occasion to wait for someone or something for a minute, an hour, a day, a week, or even a year. Can you imagine how our progenitors must feel, some of whom have perhaps been waiting for decades and even centuries for the temple work to be done for them.[37]

LDS officials exhort individual Mormons to visit the temple to perform rituals for the dead regularly. Since I serve as a pastor in a church located only a block from the Arizona temple in the city of Mesa, almost every day I drive by a parking lot full of cars left behind by Mormons performing ritual ordinances for the dead inside the temple as their act of obedience.

Many Mormons testify that the veil between the living and the dead becomes very thin in the temple. Interestingly, some Mormons say that while performing temple ordinances for the dead, they often feel the presence of the dead person in question.

Mormon Family Genealogical Research

Mormonism teaches that the salvation temple ordinances on behalf of the dead can be performed only once a dead person can be officially identified and specifically named. This official identification process is the primary purpose behind the extensive genealogical research emphasis in the LDS Church. As one Mormon writer clarifies:

> Church members are making every effort to identify every man, woman and child who ever lived on the face of the earth so that baptisms and other ordinances can be performed on their behalf. Until the Millennium, we are seeking out the dead, one name at a time.[38]

Although many people today develop their genealogies as a hobby or out of a general interest in their past heritage, faithful Mormons instead engage in a rigorous genealogical research routine in order to submit names to the temple so that ordinances for the dead can be officially completed and recorded.[39]

Mormon Temple Baptisms for the Dead

Joseph Smith initiated and strongly promoted water baptism for the dead among the Latter-day Saints:

> If we can baptize a man in the name of the Father and the Son and of the Holy Ghost for the remission of sins it is just as much our privilege to act as an agent and be baptized for the remission of sins for and in behalf of our dead kindred who have not heard the gospel or fullness of it.[40]

Smith first taught the doctrine of the baptism for the dead at a Latter-day Saints funeral in the city of Nauvoo, Illinois, on August 10, 1840, approximately ten years after the LDS Church had been started in New York. The LDS *Doctrine and Covenants Student Manual* reads:

> As early as August 10, 1840, in a powerful address at the funeral of Seymour Brunson, the Prophet introduced the doctrine of baptism for the dead to a startled congregation of Saints.[41]

The first proxy water baptisms for the dead by Latter-day Saints were performed in the Mississippi River, and the first baptisms for the dead in the unfinished Nauvoo temple were initiated on November 21, 1841.

In the early years of the LDS Church, water baptisms were performed only for direct ancestors, usually going back approximately four generations or so. Today, however, Latter-day Saints perform water baptisms for the dead not only for their deceased family members but also for any other person who has been officially identified through the LDS name-extraction program. Witnesses are required for baptisms of the dead, official records must be kept, and women are baptized for women and men are baptized for men.

The Latter-day Saints support their doctrine of proxy water baptism for the dead on a single Bible verse:[42]

> What do people mean by being baptized on behalf of the dead? If the dead are not raised at all, why are people baptized on their behalf? (1 Cor. 15:29).

In the overall context of this passage, however, Paul is not supporting, and certainly not commanding, the practice of water baptism for the dead. He simply argues that since a few in the city of Corinth were practicing it,[43] then they must believe in the resurrection of the dead, which some in Corinth were denying (see 1 Cor. 15:12).

One of the most convincing arguments against Mormonism's practice of water baptism for the dead is that there is absolutely no biblical evidence that the apostle Paul or any other New Testament leader ever engaged in or encouraged the practice himself. Total biblical silence concerning a so-called key salvation practice does not bode well for those that believe and propagate it.

Salvation for the Dead during the Mormon Millennium

Some major problems face Mormonism's teaching and practice of water baptism for the dead: multitudes of genealogical records have been lost or destroyed over the centuries; there are simply not enough Mormons and temples to perform the required ordinances for the dead; and billions upon billions of people have lived since the world began, and to perform proxy temple ordinances for all of them is simply a logistical impossibility.

How do Mormons respond to these obvious problems? Many Latter-day Saints find their answers in the future Mormon millennium. In the millennium, everything that is impossible today will be solved, as emphasized by Bruce McConkie:

> Obviously, due to the frailties, incapacities, and errors of mortal men, and because the records of past ages are often scanty and inaccurate, this great work cannot be completed for every worthy soul without assistance from on high. The millennial era is the time, primarily, when this assistance will be given by resurrected beings. Genealogical records unknown to us will then become available. Errors committed by us in sealings or other ordinances will be rectified, and all things will be arranged in proper order. Temple work will be the great work of the millennium.[44]

Mormonism seems to satisfy its internal doctrinal and practice challenges related to salvation for the dead by appealing to the fact that it will all work out somehow during the millennium—a rather convenient solution.

The Mormon Millennium

The Latter-day Saints' tenth Articles of Faith creedal statement reads, "We believe in the literal gathering of Israel and in the restoration of the Ten Tribes; that Zion (the New Jerusalem) will be built upon the American continent; that Christ will reign personally upon the earth; and, that the earth will be renewed and receive its paradisiacal glory."

According to Mormonism, following the second coming of Jesus Christ, he will rule on the earth for a millennium, or a period of a thousand years.[45] At the beginning of the millennium, the entire earth will be transformed into the paradisiacal condition that initially prevailed in the garden of Eden, at which time its inhabitants will speak the pure language spoken by Adam.[46] Satan will be bound, and there will be a new heaven and a new earth.

The millennium will be a time of righteousness and peace on the earth, and it will have two capital cities—Old Jerusalem in Palestine and New Jerusalem (Zion) in America's state of Missouri.[47]

The New Mormon World

Again, according to Mormonism, at the end of the millennium, Satan will be loosed and the great last battle of Gog and Magog will occur.[48] Led by Adam—the archangel Michael in preexistence—the hosts of heaven will defeat the armies of Satan. After the resurrection of those still dwelling in the Telestial kingdom, everyone will experience God's final judgment and be sent to his or her eternal destination in the Celestial, Terrestrial, or Telestial kingdom or eternal hell. In the end, the entire earth will be totally cleansed and become the new Celestial world inhabited exclusively by true and faithful Mormons forever.[49]

APPENDIX 1

LDS Articles of Faith

1. We believe in God, the Eternal Father, and in His Son, Jesus Christ, and in the Holy Ghost.

2. We believe that men will be punished for their own sins, and not for Adam's transgression.

3. We believe that through the Atonement of Christ, all mankind may be saved, by obedience to the laws and ordinances of the Gospel.

4. We believe that the first principles and ordinances of the Gospel are: first, Faith in the Lord Jesus Christ; second, Repentance; third, Baptism by immersion for the remission of sins; fourth, Laying on of hands for the gift of the Holy Ghost.

5. We believe that a man must be called of God, by prophecy, and by the laying on of hands by those who are in authority, to preach the Gospel and administer in the ordinances thereof.

6. We believe in the same organization that existed in the Primitive Church, namely, apostles, prophets, pastors, teachers, evangelists, and so forth.

7. We believe in the gift of tongues, prophecy, revelation, visions, healing, interpretation of tongues, and so forth.

8. We believe the Bible to be the word of God as far as it is translated correctly; we also believe the Book of Mormon to be the word of God.

9. We believe all that God has revealed, all that He does now reveal, and we believe that He will yet reveal many great and important things pertaining to the Kingdom of God.

10. We believe in the literal gathering of Israel and in the restoration of the Ten Tribes; that Zion (the New Jerusalem) will be built upon the American continent; that Christ will reign personally upon the earth; and, that the earth will be renewed and receive its paradisiacal glory.

11. We claim the privilege of worshiping Almighty God according to the dictates of our own conscience, and allow all men the same privilege, let them worship how, where, or what they may.

12. We believe in being subject to kings, presidents, rulers, and magistrates, in obeying, honoring, and sustaining the law.

13. We believe in being honest, true, chaste, benevolent, virtuous, and in doing good to all men; indeed, we may say that we follow the admonition of Paul—We believe all things, we hope all things, we have endured many things, and hope to be able to endure all things. If there is anything virtuous, lovely, or of good report or praiseworthy, we seek after these things.

LDS Organizational Structure

General Administration

President and Prophet. The President of the church is the LDS prophet, seer, and revelator, the most senior living apostle, the only person on the earth who receives revelation to guide the LDS Church, and presides over the entire church.

First Presidency. The First Presidency is the highest governing body of the LDS Church, and is composed of the President of the church and his two counselors.

Quorum of the Twelve Apostles. The members of the Quorum of the Twelve Apostles are also prophets, seers, and revelators acting under the direction of the First Presidency.

apostles. The LDS Church has fifteen apostles, consisting of the members of the First Presidency and the Quorum of the Twelve Apostles.

prophets. The LDS Church believes that the members of the First Presidency and the Quorum of the Twelve Apostles are prophets.

Presiding Bishopric. The Presiding Bishopric is the presidency of the Aaronic Priesthood throughout the LDS Church and has two counselors. It serves under the direction of the First Presidency to administer the temporal affairs of the church.

Area Administration

An area is the largest geographic division of the LDS Church. The First Presidency assigns the Presidency of the Seventy to supervise selected areas of the church under the direction of the Quorum of the Twelve Apostles. In other areas of the church, the First Presidency assigns Area Presidencies to preside.

Quorums of the Seventy. The members of the Quorums of the Seventy work under the direction of the Twelve Apostles, and are the leadership of seven men who are called to serve as the Presidency of the Seventy. Members of the First and Second Quorums of the Seventy are designated General Authorities, and they may be called to serve anywhere in the world.

Area Presidency. An Area Presidency consists of a president, who is usually assigned from the First or Second Quorum of the Seventy, and two counselors. Area Presidencies serve under the direction of the First Presidency, the Quorum of the Twelve, and the Presidency of the Seventy.

Area Seventies. Some men are ordained to the office of Seventy but do not serve as General Authorities. They are called *Area Seventies*, and they are assigned to quorums other than the First and Second Quorums of the Seventy, according to geographic location. Their jurisdiction is limited to the general region in which they live.

Local Administration

wards. Members of the LDS Church are organized into congregations. Large congregations are called *wards*. Each ward is presided over by a bishop, assisted by two counselors.

branches. Small congregations are called *branches*. Each branch is presided over by a branch president, assisted by two counselors. A branch may be organized when at least two member families live in an area and one of the members is a worthy Melchizedek Priesthood holder or a worthy priest in the Aaronic Priesthood. A stake, mission, or district presidency organizes and supervises the branch. A branch can develop into a ward if it is located within a stake.

stakes. Most geographic areas where the LDS Church is organized are divided into stakes. There are usually five to twelve wards and branches in a stake. Each stake is presided over by a stake president, assisted by two counselors. The stake president is under the oversight of the Presidency of the Seventy or the Area Presidency.

missions. A mission is a unit of the LDS Church that normally covers an area much larger than that of a stake. Each mission is presided over by a mission president, assisted by two counselors. Mission presidents are directly accountable to General Authorities.

districts. Just as a branch is a smaller version of a ward, a district is a smaller version of a stake. A district is organized when enough branches are located in an area. A district president is called to preside over it, assisted by two counselors. The district president reports to the mission presidency. A district can develop into a stake.

Priesthoods

Through the Mormon priesthood God's eternal power and authority is active. Through the priesthood God created and governs the heavens and the earth. God gives priesthood authority to worthy male members of the LDS Church so that they can act in his name for the salvation of his children. Priesthood holders can be authorized to preach the gospel, administer the ordinances of salvation, and govern the kingdom of God on the earth.

Melchizedek Priesthood for Adult Men

Through the authority of the Melchizedek Priesthood, the LDS Church leaders guide the church. This greater priesthood was given to Adam and has been on the earth whenever the Lord has revealed his gospel. It was taken from the earth during the great apostasy, but it was restored in 1829, when the apostles Peter, James, and John conferred it upon Joseph Smith and Oliver Cowdery.

high council. Twelve high priests sit as a high council under the direction of a stake presidency and minister by teaching, training, and supervising stake personnel or programs. The high council also convenes as a disciplinary council in cases of serious personal transgression.

patriarch. A patriarch is one who is ordained to give special blessings to members of the church. Patriarchal blessings include a declaration of a person's lineage in the house of Israel and contain personal counsel from the Lord.

high priest. A high priest has the right to officiate in the church. Stake presidents, mission presidents, high councilors, bishops and their counselors, and other leaders of the church are ordained as high priests.

elder. *Elder* is used as a title for male missionaries or General Authorities of the church. Elders have authority to bestow the gift of the Holy Ghost by the laying on of hands and to bestow priesthood blessings.

Aaronic Priesthood for Young Men

Worthy male members may receive the Aaronic Priesthood beginning at age twelve. These young men, typically ages twelve to seventeen, receive opportunities to participate in sacred priesthood ordinances and give service.

bishop. A man who has been ordained and set apart as the presiding high priest for a ward is a bishop. He has overall responsibility for ministering the temporal and spiritual affairs of the congregation.

priest. A worthy young man may be ordained as a priest when he is sixteen years of age or older. A newly baptized adult man is also normally ordained as a priest shortly following his baptism. Some of a priest's responsibilities are to administer or bless the sacrament and to preach the gospel to the members.

teacher. A teacher serves as instructor by conducting classes and presenting gospel lessons.

deacon. A boy is normally ordained as a deacon when he is twelve years of age or older. Some of a deacon's responsibilities are to pass the sacrament and collect fast offerings.

LDS Terminology

This appendix contains basic and generalized Mormon terminology collected from LDS resources. For further clarification on Mormon terminology, see www.lds.org (A–Z Index) and www.mormon.org (Glossary). But realize that many of these definitions often lack clarity and specifics.

agency. The ability and freedom to choose good or evil.

apostasy. A condition of spiritual withdrawal from the Father in heaven. A period of time when the priesthood and the gospel of Jesus Christ in its fullness were not on the earth.

atonement of Jesus Christ. To atone is to suffer the penalty for sins, thereby removing the effects of sin from the repentant sinner and allowing him or her to be reconciled to God. Jesus Christ was the only one capable of carrying out the atonement for all humankind. Because of his atonement, all people will be resurrected, and those who obey his gospel will merit eternal life with God.

baptisms for the dead. Jesus Christ taught that baptism is essential to the salvation of all who have lived on earth (see John 3:5). Many people, however, have died without being baptized. Others were baptized without proper authority. Because God is merciful, he has prepared a way for all people to receive the blessings of baptism. By performing proxy baptisms in behalf of those who have died, church members offer these blessings to deceased ancestors. Individuals can then choose to accept or reject what has been done in their behalf.

Celestial kingdom. The highest of the three degrees or kingdoms of glory in heaven, in which one is in the presence of the heavenly Father and Jesus Christ.

eternal life. *Eternal life* is the phrase used in Scripture to define the quality of life that the Eternal Father lives. Eternal life, or exaltation, is to live in God's presence and to continue as families. Like immortality, this gift is made possible through the atonement of Jesus Christ. To inherit eternal life, however, requires "obedience to the laws and ordinances of the Gospel" (Articles of Faith 1:3).

excommunication. A disciplinary process used only in extreme situations, excommunication includes removal of an individual's name from the records of the church. Excommunicated individuals have the opportunity to return and have their church membership restored through the process of repentance and baptism by immersion for the remission of sins.

foreordination. In the premortal spirit-world, God appointed certain spirits to fulfill specific missions during their mortal lives. This is called *foreordination*. Foreordination does not guarantee that individuals will receive certain callings or responsibilities. Such opportunities come in this life as a result of the righteous exercise of agency, just as foreordination came as a result of righteousness in the premortal existence.

grace. Through the grace of the Lord Jesus, made possible by his atoning sacrifice, humankind will be raised in immortality, every person receiving his or her body from the grave in a condition of everlasting life. This grace is an enabling power that allows men and women to lay hold on Christ and repent of their sins, receive strength and assistance to do good efforts, and receive eternal life and exaltation.

gospel. The gospel is the heavenly Father's plan of happiness. The Prophet Joseph Smith said, "The first principles and ordinances of the Gospel are: first, Faith in the Lord Jesus Christ; second, Repentance; third, Baptism by immersion for the remission of sins; fourth, Laying on of hands for the gift of the Holy Ghost" (Articles of Faith 1:4).

hell. Latter-day revelations speak of hell in at least two ways. First, it is another name for spirit-prison, a temporary place in the postmortal world for those who died without a knowledge of the truth or those who were disobedient in mortality. Second, it is the permanent location of Satan and his followers and the sons of perdition, who are not redeemed by the atonement of Jesus Christ.

laying on of hands. The laying on of hands is the procedure revealed by the Lord for performing many priesthood ordinances, such as confirmation, ordination, setting members apart to serve in callings, administering to the sick, and giving other priesthood blessings.

ordinances. In the church, an ordinance is a sacred, formal act performed by the authority of the priesthood. Some ordinances are essential to one's exaltation. These ordinances are called *saving ordinances*. They include baptism, confirmation, ordination to the Melchizedek Priesthood (for men), the temple endowment, and the marriage sealing.

original sin. Because of the fall of Adam and Eve, all people live in a fallen condition, separated from God and subject to physical death. But they are not condemned by what many call the *original sin*. In other words, people are not accountable for Adam's transgression in the garden of Eden.

paradise. Paradise is that part of the spirit-world in which the righteous spirits who have departed from this life await the resurrection of the body. It is a condition of happiness and peace.

pre-earth life. A person's life before being born on this earth is his or her pre-earth life. In the pre-earth life, people lived in the presence of the heavenly Father as his spirit-children. They did not have physical bodies.

priesthood. The priesthood is the eternal power and authority of God. Through the priesthood God created and governs the heavens and the earth. God gives priesthood authority to worthy male members of the church so that they can act in his name for the salvation of his children. Priesthood holders can be authorized to preach the gospel, administer the ordinances of salvation, and govern the kingdom of God on the earth.

restoration of the gospel. When Jesus Christ was on the earth, he established his church among his followers. After his crucifixion and the deaths of his apostles, the fullness of the gospel was taken from the earth because of widespread apostasy. Through the Prophet Joseph Smith, the Father in heaven and his Son Jesus Christ restored the fullness of the gospel. The true church of Jesus Christ is on the earth again. Because of the restoration, the teachings and ordinances necessary for salvation are available to all people.

salvation. In the doctrine of the Church of Jesus Christ of Latter-day Saints, the terms *saved* and *salvation* have various meanings. As used in Romans 10:9–10, the words *saved* and *salvation* signify a covenant relationship with Jesus Christ. Through this covenant relationship, followers of Christ are assured of salvation from the eternal consequences of sin if they are obedient.

sealing. Sealing is an ordinance performed in the temple eternally uniting a husband and wife, or children and their parents.

spirits. Each individual is a spirit-child of the heavenly Father and existed as a spirit before this life on earth. During this life, the spirit of the individual is housed in a physical body, which was born of mortal parents.

spirit-world. Human spirits go to the spirit-world between death and resurrection.

Telestial kingdom. The Telestial kingdom is the lowest of the three degrees or kingdoms of glory in heaven.

temples. Temples are literally houses of the Lord. They are holy places of worship where individuals make sacred covenants with God. Because making covenants with God is such a solemn responsibility, individuals cannot enter the temple to receive their endowments or be sealed in marriage for eternity until they have fully prepared themselves and been members of the church for at least a year. Throughout history, the Lord has commanded his people to build temples. The church is working to build temples all over the world to make temple blessings more available for a greater number of the heavenly Father's children.

Terrestrial kingdom. The Terrestrial kingdom is the middle degree or kingdom of the three degrees of glory in heaven.

vicarious work. Ordinance work done on behalf of those who are deceased is vicarious work.

water baptism. Baptism by immersion in water by one having priesthood authority is the first saving ordinance of the gospel and is necessary for an individual to become a member of the Church of Jesus Christ of Latter-day Saints and to receive eternal salvation.

Zion. The word *Zion* has various meanings in the Scriptures. The most general definition of the word is "the pure in heart." *Zion* is often used in this way to refer to the Lord's people or to the church and its stakes. It has also been used to refer to specific geographical locations.

Select Resources

Internet

Mormon

Brigham Young University: www.byu.edu

Brigham Young's *Journal of Discourses*: www.JournalOfDiscourses. org/

Encyclopedia of Mormonism: www.lib.byu.edu/Macmillan/

FAIR Wiki: www.fairwiki.org/

Foundation for Apologetic Information & Research (FAIR): www. fairlds.org

Hill Cumorah: www.HillCumorah.org

Joseph Smith: www.JosephSmith.net

Joseph Smith, *History of the Church* (7 vols.): http://byustudies2.byu. edu/hc/hcpgs/hc.aspx?HC=/hc/1/4.html&A=10

Joseph Smith Translation: http://scriptures.lds.org/en/jst/contents

Journal of Discourses: www.journalofdiscourses.org

LDS Church Educational System: www.ldsces.org

LDS Newsroom: www.newsroom.lds.org

LDS Places to Visit: www.lds.org/placestovisit

LDS Scriptures Online: www.scriptures.lds.org

LDS Today: www.ldstoday.com

LDS Web Site (official): www.lds.org

Mormon Church History Maps: http://scriptures.lds.org/en /chmaps/contents

Mormon Trail: www.mormontrail.net

Mormon Web Site: www.mormon.org

Nauvoo: www.nauvoo.com

The Neil A. Maxwell Institute for Religious Scholarship (FARMS): www.farms.byu.edu

True to the Faith: http://lds.org/languages/youthmaterials/trueTo-Thefaith/TrueFaith_000.pdf

Non-Mormon

Utah Lighthouse Ministries, Jerald and Sandra Tanner: www.utlm. org

Mormonism Research Ministry: www.mrm.org

Mormon Wiki: www.mormonwiki.org

Institute for Religious Research: www.irr.org

Books

Mormon

Blomberg, Craig, and Stephen Robinson. *How Wide the Divide? A Mormon & an Evangelical in Conversation.* Downers Grove, IL: InterVarsity Press, 1997.

Bushman, Richard Lyman. *Joseph Smith: Rough Stone Rolling: A Cultural Biography of Mormonism's Founder.* New York: Vintage Books, 2005.

Hopkins, Richard R. *Biblical Mormonism: Responding to Evangelical Criticism of LDS Theology.* Bountiful, UT: Horizon, 1994.

LDS Church Educational System. *Book of Mormon: Student Manual, Religion 121 and 122.* Salt Lake City: The Church of Jesus Christ of Latter-day Saints, 1996.

————. *Church History in the Fulness of Times, Religion 341–43*. Salt Lake City: The Church of Jesus Christ of Latter-day Saints, 1993.

————. *Doctrine and Covenants: Student Manual, Religion 324 and 325*. Salt Lake City: The Church of Jesus Christ of Latter-day Saints, 1981.

————. *Doctrines of the Gospel: Student Manual, Religion 231 and 232*. Salt Lake City: The Church of Jesus Christ of Latter-day Saints, 1986.

Lee, Rex E. *What Do Mormons Believe?* Salt Lake City: Deseret, 1992.

McConkie, Bruce R. *Mormon Doctrine*, 2d ed. Salt Lake City: Bookcraft, 1966.

Millet, Robert L. *A Different Jesus? The Christ of the Latter-day Saints*. Grand Rapids, MI: Eerdmans, 2005.

————. *Getting at the Truth*. Salt Lake City: Deseret, 2004.

————. *Grace Works*. Salt Lake City: Deseret, 2003.

————. *Lost and Found*. Salt Lake City: Deseret, 2001.

————. *The Mormon Faith: A New Look at Christianity*. Salt Lake City: Shadow Mountain, 1998.

Millet, Robert, and Roger Keller. *Salvation in Christ: Comparative Christian Views*. Provo, UT: BYU Religious Studies Center, 2005.

Newell, Coke. *Latter Days: A Guided Tour through Six Billion Years of Mormonism*. New York: St. Martin's Press, 2000.

Robinson, Stephen E. *Are Mormons Christians?* Salt Lake City: Bookcraft, 1991.

Robinson, Stephen E., and Dean Garrett. *A Commentary on the Doctrine and Covenants* (3 vols.). Utah: Deseret. 2001–2004.

Smith, Joseph. "King Follett Sermon." In *History of the Church*, 6:302–17.

Smith, Joseph Fielding. *Doctrines of Salvation*. Salt Lake City: Cannon and Sons, 1891.

Young, Brigham. *Discourses of Brigham Young*. Compiled by John A. Widtoe. Salt Lake City: Deseret, 1978.

Non-Mormon Books

Beckwith, Francis J., Carl Mosser, and Paul Owen, eds. *The New Mormon Challenge: Responding to the Latest Defenses of a Fast-Growing Movement*. Grand Rapids, MI: Zondervan, 2002.

Blomberg, Craig, and Stephen Robinson. *How Wide the Divide? A Mormon & an Evangelical in Conversation*. Wheaton, IL: Inter-Varsity Press, 1997.

Davies, Douglas. *An Introduction to Mormonism*. Cambridge, United Kingdom: Cambridge University Press, 2003.

McKeever, Bill, and Eric Johnson. *Mormonism 101*. Grand Rapids, MI: Baker Books, 2000.

Ostling, Richard and Joan. *Mormon America: The Power and the Promise*. New York: HarperSanFrancisco, 1999.

Shipps, Jan. *Mormonism: The Story of a New Religious Tradition*. Champaign, IL: The University of Illinois Press, 1987.

———. *Sojourner in the Promised Land: Forty Years among the Mormons*. Champaign, IL: The University of Illinois Press, 2000.

NOTES

1. Introduction

1. Craig Blomberg and Stephen Robinson, *How Wide the Divide? A Mormon & an Evangelical in Conversation* (Downers Grove, IL: InterVarsity Press, 1997), 14–15.

2. Ibid., 14.

3. Ibid., 140.

4. Robert L. Millet, *A Different Jesus? The Christ of the Latter-day Saints* (Grand Rapids, MI: Eerdmans, 2005), 61.

5. Blomberg and Robinson, *How Wide the Divide?* 57.

6. Ibid., 58.

7. Ibid., 59.

8. *Book of Mormon*: 1 Nephi 13:25–29; *Doctrine and Covenants* 73, 76; LDS Church Educational System, *Doctrine and Covenants: Student Manual, Religion 324 and 325* (Salt Lake City: The Church of Jesus Christ of Latter-day Saints, 1981), 153–54, 158.

9. Primarily www.lds.org and www.Mormon.org.

10. LDS Church Educational System, The Church of Jesus Christ of Latter-day Saints, www.ldsces.org.

11. *Encyclopedia of Mormonism* (New York: Macmillan, 1992), www.lib.byu.edu/Macmillan.

Chapter 1: Joseph Smith: The Restorer of the True Gospel?

1. Some Mormons I conversed with insist that God would have chosen another latter-day prophet if Joseph Smith had failed for some reason. But Mormons do not simply admire Joseph Smith as Christians respect Billy Graham; they have elevated him to the biblical status of Abraham, Moses, Peter, and Paul. See Robert L. Millet, *A Different Jesus? The Christ of the Latter-day Saints* (Grand Rapids, MI: Eerdmans, 2005), 157. Latter-day Saints exalt Joseph Smith to a status of greatness that is hard for Christians to imagine. Mormons believe Smith was a pre-existent spirit-man who ranked with Adam and Abraham. See *Pearl of Great Price*: Abraham 3:22–23; Bruce R. McConkie, *Mormon Doctrine*, 2d ed. (Salt Lake City: Bookcraft, 1966), 396. Mormons believe that Smith, as second only to Jesus Christ, has done more for the salvation of men in this world than any other man who has ever lived on earth. See *Doctrine and Covenants* (hereafter DC) 135:3. In their eyes, Joseph Smith is greater than any Old Testament prophet or New Testament apostle, including Moses, Abraham, Paul, and John. See LDS Church Educational System, *Doctrine and Covenants: Student Manual, Religion 324 and 325* (Salt Lake City: The Church of Jesus Christ of Latter-day Saints, 1981), 349. Although Mormons do not worship Joseph Smith, they do acclaim his status of preexistent greatness and latter-day calling to a level of superiority that is unprecedented in the history of Christianity. One of the best biographies on Joseph Smith has been written by

LDS Richard Lyman Bushman, *Joseph Smith: Rough Stone Rolling: A Cultural Biography of Mormonism's Founder* (New York: Vintage Books, 2005).

2. In 1638, Robert Smith—Joseph Smith's third great-grandfather—emigrated from England to Boston. The Smith genealogy records five generations that lived in and around Topsfield Township of northeastern Massachusetts, approximately twenty miles north of Boston. Joseph Smith Sr. was born in Topsfield on July 12, 1771, to Asahel Smith and his wife, Mary. After marrying Lucy Mack, Joseph Smith Sr. moved to the town of Sharon, Windsor County, Vermont, where he began working his father-in-law's farm.

3. The Palmyra temple sits today on a high ridge at the east end of the original hundred acres of the Joseph Smith Sr. farm in Manchester Township, New York, and was dedicated by the LDS Church on April 6, 2000—the 170th anniversary of the organization of the Mormon Church.

4. Although the 1820 date of the First Vision is the official position of the LDS Church, there are many historical questions concerning whether this date and Smith's description of his First Vision are accurate.

5. *Pearl of Great Price*: Joseph Smith—History.

6. There were many wild-eyed preachers in western New York, including Lorenzo Dow (nicknamed "Crazy Dow"), after whom Brigham Young's older brother was named, and unwashed evangelist Isaac Bullard, who ran around draped in bearskin yelling his message of free love. And it was here that Charles Finney began his evangelistic preaching crusades in 1824 and 1825.

7. Actually, early Christian restorationist movements did use the motto "The Bible is our creed." Although many Mormons take pride in rejecting historical Christian creeds, they have creeds themselves.

8. Roger E. Olson, *Armininan Theology: Myths and Realities* (Downers Grove, IL: InterVarsity Press, 2006), 206.

9. Mark A. Noll, *A History of Christianity in the United States and Canada* (Grand Rapids, MI: Eerdmans, 1992), 151–52, 237–38.

10. See Craig Blomberg's excellent evaluation of early Mormonism in Francis J. Beckwith, Carl Mosser, and Paul Owen, eds., *The New Mormon Challenge: Responding to the Latest Defenses of a Fast-Growing Movement* (Grand Rapids, MI: Zondervan, 2002), 322–24; Stephen E. Robinson, *Are Mormons Christians?* (Salt Lake City: Bookcraft, 1991), 18; Craig L. Blomberg and Stephen E. Robinson, *How Wide the Divide? A Mormon & an Evangelical in Conversation* (Downers Grove, IL: InterVarsity Press, 1997), 52.

11. Although the Smith family belonged to the Presbyterian Church, apparently fourteen-year-old Joseph Jr. was personally attracted to the Methodists.

12. Joseph Smith—History, 1:5–10.

13. Bushman, *Joseph Smith*, 37; LDS Church Educational System, *Church History in the Fulness of Times, Religion 341–43* (Salt Lake City: The Church of Jesus Christ of Latter-day Saints, 1993), 31. It is recorded that Joseph Smith stated that he became very serious about Christianity at the age of twelve.

14. Bushman, *Joseph Smith*, 39; *Church History in the Fulness of Times*, 33. This is the first time that Joseph Smith prayed out loud.

15. *Church History in the Fulness of Times*, 33; Bushman, *Joseph Smith*, 40; Joseph Smith—History, 1:15. Joseph Smith describes his First Vision as a deliverance experience.

16. Although this is the official LDS position, Joseph Smith actually did not indicate that he saw two personages until 1835, and they were not identified as the Father and the Son until 1838.

17. Bushman, *Joseph Smith*, 36. Joseph Smith Sr. probably had a strong influence on Joseph Smith Jr., since it is recorded that he had numerous visions before and after Joseph Smith Jr.'s First Vision experience.

18. Ibid., 39–40.

19. Richard L. Anderson, "Joseph Smith's Testimony of the First Vision," *Ensign*, April 1996, 10–21.

20. Joseph Smith, www.JosephSmith. net. See under "Mission of the Prophet: The First Vision."

21. Gordon B. Hinckley, "What Are People Asking about us?" LDS General Conference, October 1998, www.lightplanet. com/mormons/conferences/98_oct/index. htm.

22. www.JosephSmith.net; Richard and Joan Ostling, *Mormon America: The Power and the Promise* (New York: HarperSanFrancisco, 1999), 24. The sacred grove of Joseph Smith's First Vision is owned today by the LDS Church.

23. Joseph Smith—History, 1:28.

24. *Church History in the Fulness of Times*, 37.

25. Bushman, *Joseph Smith*, 48–52.

26. The hundreds of Indian burial mounds scattered throughout western New York were of great interest to early European settlers. As a result, an extensive written folklore emerged, speculating on the origins of ancient American Indian civilizations. Mormons believe that American Indians are the direct ancestors of the *Book of Mormon*'s Lamanite people and thus are also direct descendants of Israelites.

27. Bushman, *Joseph Smith*, 51.

28. Ibid., 49.

29. *Book of Mormon*: Testimony of the Prophet Joseph Smith.

30. www.HillCumorah.org. A twelve-meter granite-and-bronze monument to Moroni stands on Hill Cumorah in New York today.

31. Because this book was made of pure gold—although some Mormons say it was an alloy of copper and gold and so simply had the appearance of gold—Moroni warned Joseph Jr. that it must not be sold in order for him to become rich.

32. Ex. 28:30; 1 Sam. 28:6; Ezra 2:63.

33. *Book of Mormon*: Mormon 9:32–34; LDS Church Educational System, *Book of Mormon: Student Manual, Religion 121 and 122* (Salt Lake City: The Church of Jesus Christ of Latter-day Saints, 1996), 4.

34. Joseph Smith, *History of the Church*, 4:537.

35. www.HillCumorah.org. The Hill Cumorah is located between the villages of Palmyra and Manchester and each summer is the site of an outdoor Mormon pageant featuring a cast of over six hundred that apparently attracts audiences of up to a hundred thousand each year.

36. Bushman, *Joseph Smith*, 45.

37. Testimony of the Prophet Joseph Smith.

38. *Encyclopedia of Mormonism*, s.v. "Angel Moroni Statue" (New York: Macmillan, 1992), 39.

39. Ostling and Ostling, *Mormon America*, 25.

40. Joseph Smith—History, 1:59.

41. *Church History in the Fulness of Times*, 45.

42. The LDS seventh Article of Faith reads, "We believe in the gift of tongues, prophecy, revelation, visions, healing, interpretation of tongues, and so forth." There is no mention of a gift of translation here either. See *DC* 8:1–3 concerning the spirit of revelation and translation requested by Oliver Cowdery; *Doctrine and Covenants Student Manual*, 18.

43. Bushman, *Joseph Smith*, 71–74.

44. *DC* 1:29; *DC* 3, 5 (Martin Harris); *DC* 6 (Oliver Cowdery); *Doctrine and Covenants Student Manual*, 3, 9, 12, 14, 28; *DC* 13.

45. PBS television special *The Mormons*, 2007.

46. Bushman, *Joseph Smith*, 105.

47. Ibid., 130.

48. *Church History in the Fulness of Times*, 61.

49. Ibid., 32. There were apparently eleven special witnesses to the *Book of*

Mormon before its publication. Of these witnesses, Martin Harris, Oliver Cowdery, David, John, and Jacob Whitmer, and Hiram Page all later left or were excommunicated from the Mormon Church.

50. DC 7; *Doctrine and Covenants Student Manual*, 17.

51. DC 13; *Doctrine and Covenants Student Manual*, 28. The story concerning the visit of John the Baptist, however, was not told until many years later. See Bushman, *Joseph Smith*, 75.

52. DC 7.

53. Joseph Smith—History, 1:69; DC 13; *Doctrine and Covenants Student Manual*, 28.

54. DC 7:7; 27:12–13; 128:20; *Church History in the Fulness of Times*, 56. The keys of the kingdom given to Joseph Smith were the keys of the First Presidency that Mormons say Peter, James, and John received from Jesus on the Mount of Transfiguration.

55. DC 2; *Doctrine and Covenants Student Manual*, 6; *Church History in the Fulness of Times*, 6–8.

56. *Church History in the Fulness of Times*, 64.

57. Bushman, *Joseph Smith*, 109. The exact location of the LDS Church's first organization is disputed.

58. DC 20:1. God revealed to Joseph Smith the exact day on which the new latter-day Mormon Church should be organized. See *Church History in the Fulness of Times*, 64. The LDS Church reconstructed Whitmer's log home in 1980.

59. *Church History in the Fulness of Times*, 70–71.

60. DC 21:1–2; *Doctrine and Covenants Student Manual*, 43.

61. DC 21:5.

62. Ibid., 28; *Doctrine and Covenants Student Manual*, 57–59.

Chapter 2: Joseph Smith's Mormons Move West

1. *Pearl of Great Price*: Moses 7:19–21.

2. *Book of Mormon*: Ether 13:2–3; 3 Nephi 20:22.

3. *Doctrine and Covenants* (hereafter DC) 29:7–9.

4. Ibid., 21.

5. Ibid., 22.

6. Ibid., 24.

7. LDS Church Educational System, *Church History in the Fulness of Times, Religion 341–43* (Salt Lake City: The Church of Jesus Christ of Latter-day Saints, 1993), 70.

8. DC 3, 7–9, 13, 76.

9. Richard Lyman Bushman, *Joseph Smith: Rough Stone Rolling: A Cultural Biography of Mormonism's Founder* (New York: Vintage Books, 2005), 133–42.

10. DC 28:1–7.

11. Ibid., 3:18, 20; 10:48.

12. Ibid., 32–33.

13. *Book of Mormon*: Alma 9:17.

14. DC 28:8; 30; 32.

15. *Church History in the Fulness of Times*, 85.

16. Ibid., 82.

17. DC 35.

18. Ibid., 37, 38:31–32.

19. Ibid., 37:1; LDS Church Educational System, *Doctrine and Covenants: Student Manual, Religion 324 and 325* (Salt Lake City: The Church of Jesus Christ of Latter-day Saints, 1981), 74.

20. DC 28:9.

21. www.lds.org. See under "About the Church: Places to Visit."

22. In 1979, the Mormon Church purchased the Newel Whitney store and restored it. It was officially dedicated on August 25, 1984.

23. DC 42.

24. Ibid., 41; *Doctrine and Covenants Student Manual*, 81.

25. DC 41.

26. Ibid., 42, 51. For the list of revelations related to Joseph Smith's Law of Consecration, see *Church History in the Fulness of Times*, 98.

27. *Encyclopedia of Mormonism,* s.v. "Consecration" (New York: Macmillan, 1992), 312–14.

28. DC 41, 43.

29. Ibid., 43, 50, 52.

30. Bushman, *Joseph Smith,* 157–60.

31. DC 44.

32. Ibid., 52.

33. Ibid., 52, 55–56.

34. Ibid., 52: 2, 42.

35. Ibid., 57; *Church History in the Fulness of Times,* 106.

36. DC 57:1–3.

37. Brigham Young, *Journal of Discourses* 8:195, www.journalofdiscourses.org.

38. DC 47:3–5; 58:37, 49–52; 63:27; *Church History in the Fulness of Times,* 107.

39. *Church History in the Fulness of Times,* 188.

40. Bushman, *Joseph Smith,* 219–22.

41. DC 52:2.

42. *Church History in the Fulness of Times,* 108.

43. DC 65.

44. DC 76 and 77 are a direct product of Joseph Smith's Bible revisions, and many other of his revelations could be easily sighted. See *Church History in the Fulness of Times,* 118–19.

45. DC 86.

46. Joseph Smith, *History of the Church,* 1:398.

47. DC 107:23, 93.

48. Ibid., 88.

49. Ibid., 93.

50. Ibid., 67, 69–70.

51. *Church History in the Fulness of Times,* 159.

52. Ibid., 164.

53. DC 88:119.

54. Smith, *History,* 2:428.

55. The Kirtland temple is owned today by the Restored Latter-day Saints. *Church History in the Fulness of Times,* 167; DC 110.

56. DC 111.

57. *Doctrine and Covenants Student Manual,* 277.

58. *Church History in the Fulness of Times,* 171.

59. Ibid., 177.

60. Bushman, *Joseph Smith,* 322.

61. *Church History in the Fulness of Times,* 181; DC 97.

62. DC 105.

63. Ibid., 115:4.

64. Ibid., 113; *Doctrine and Covenants Student Manual,* 283.

65. DC 119.

66. *Encyclopedia of Mormonism,* s.v. "Adam-Ondi-Ahman," 19–20.

67. DC 116.

68. Bruce R. McConkie, *Mormon Doctrine,* 2d ed. (Salt Lake City: Bookcraft, 1966), 19–20.

69. Ibid., 19–21.

70. DC 121–23.

71. Richard and Joan Ostling, *Mormon America: The Power and the Promise* (New York: HarperSanFrancisco, 1999), 194.

72. DC 124:29–36; 127–128.

73. Ibid., 130:22.

74. Ibid., 132.

75. "The discourse may be one of the Prophet's greatest sermons because of its comprehensive doctrinal teachings." *Encyclopedia of Mormonism,* s.v. "King Follett Discourse."

76. Ibid., s.v. "Council of Fifty," 326–27.

77. DC 135.

Chapter 3: From Joseph Smith to Salt Lake City

1. LDS Church Educational System, *Church History in the Fulness of Times, Religion 341–43* (Salt Lake City: The Church of Jesus Christ of Latter-day Saints, 1993), 291.

2. Community of Christ, www.cofchrist.org.

3. Not all Mormons were involved in the initial migration west from Illinois to Utah. By the late summer of 1846, nearly twelve thousand Mormons were still scattered throughout the Midwest.

4. July 24 each year is the Pioneer Day celebration in Utah.

5. *Book of Mormon*: Ether 2:3.

6. A *company* is a group of separate organized travelers led by a company captain.

7. The borders of the Deseret Territory included what are now Utah, Nevada, the western region of New Mexico and Colorado, and Arizona.

8. Richard and Joan Ostling, *Mormon America: The Power and the Promise* (New York: HarperSanFrancisco, 1999), 50.

9. Ibid., 54. *September Dawn*, starring Jon Voight, is a major movie about the Mountain Meadows Massacre, one of the darkest chapters in Mormon history.

10. Ostling and Ostling, *Mormon America*, 58.

11. Ibid., 46.

12. Fred Collier, *Unpublished Revelations of the Prophets and Presidents of the Church of Jesus Christ of Latter-day Saints* (n.p.: Collier's Publishing, 1981), 1:145–46.

Chapter 4: The One and Only True Church on Earth

1. www.lds.org. See under "A–Z Index: Restoration of the Gospel."

2. Bruce R. McConkie, *Mormon Doctrine*, 2d ed. (Salt Lake City: Bookcraft, 1966), 415–16.

3. Ibid., 670, 136.

4. *Pearl of Great Price*: Joseph Smith—History, 1:19.

5. Stephen E. Robinson, *Are Mormons Christians?* (Salt Lake City: Bookcraft, 1991), 34.

6. Ibid., chap. 1.

7. Robert L. Millet, *A Different Jesus? The Christ of the Latter-day Saints* (Grand Rapids, MI: Eerdmans, 2005), 43–44.

8. *Doctrine and Covenants* (hereafter *DC*) 86:3.

9. LDS Church Educational System, *Book of Mormon: Student Manual, Religion 121 and 122* (Salt Lake City: The Church of Jesus Christ of Latter-day Saints, 1996), 14.

10. See Matt. 24:4–24; John 16:2–3; Acts 20; 1 Cor. 1:10–13; 2 Cor. 11:4–13;

Gal. 1:6–8; 2 Thess. 2:1–12; 1 Tim. 4:1–3; 2 Tim. 3:1–13; 4:3–4; Titus 1:10–16; 2 Peter 2:1–3; 3:3; 1 John 2:18–19; 3 John 9–10; Jude 3–4, 17–18; Revelation 2–3; 13:4–8.

11. *Book of Mormon*: 1 Nephi 26, 135.

12. Robinson, *Are Mormons Christians?* 38, 40; *Encyclopedia of Mormonism*, s.v. "Apostasy" (New York: Macmillan, 1992), 56–57.

13. Millet, *A Different Jesus?* 39; Robinson, *Are Mormons Christians?* 34; LDS Church Educational System, *Doctrine and Covenants: Student Manual, Religion 324 and 325* (Salt Lake City: The Church of Jesus Christ of Latter-day Saints, 1981), 28.

14. Stephen Robinson, "Nephi's Great and Abominable Church," in *Journal of Book of Mormon Studies* (Provo, Utah: FARMS, 1998): 32–39.

15. Mormonism interprets Matthew 16:18 with a few major twists. Mormons interpret the "rock" as "revelation" and not Peter's confession of Jesus the Christ, and "hell" as referring to spirit-prison in the spirit-world and not eternal hell.

16. Most Christians believe that even during the most corrupt medieval period of the Roman Catholic Church, there were still true and genuine followers of Jesus Christ.

17. Robinson, *Are Mormons Christians?* 35.

18. Millet, *A Different Jesus?* 42–43.

19. Christians must always be aware that the current LDS top church leaders determine both the content and the method or hermeneutic of Mormon thought and practice. Current revelation always supersedes past revelation, even if canonized in Mormonism's Standard Works.

20. Craig Blomberg and Stephen Robinson, *How Wide the Divide? A Mormon & an Evangelical in Conversation* (Downers Grove, IL: InterVarsity Press, 1997), 61.

21. Robinson, *Are Mormons Christians?* 34.

22. McConkie, *Mormon Doctrine*, 415; *Encyclopedia of Mormonism*, s.v. "Authority," 88–89.

23. See Robert Millet, *The Mormon Faith: A New Look at Christianity* (Salt Lake City: Shadow Mountain, 1998), chap. 8.

24. www.lds.org. See under "A–Z Index: Priesthood."

25. *Doctrine and Covenants Student Manual*, 433; McConkie, *Mormon Doctrine*, 683.

26. *DC* 107:1.

27. Rex E. Lee, *What Do Mormons Believe?* (Salt Lake City: Deseret, 1992), 40.

28. Millet, *A Different Jesus?* 203.

29. *DC* 107:14.

30. www.lds.org. See under "A–Z Index: Aaronic Priesthood."

31. Heb. 7:11; *DC* 107:2–4.

32. *DC* 107:2–4; *Book of Mormon*: Alma 13:14–19.

33. www.lds.org. See under "A–Z Index: Melchizedek Priesthood."

34. *DC* 107:8, 18.

35. McConkie, *Mormon Doctrine*, 479.

36. Francis J. Beckwith, Carl Mosser, and Paul Owen, eds., *The New Mormon Challenge: Responding to the Latest Defenses of a Fast-Growing Movement* (Grand Rapids, MI: Zondervan, 2002), chap. 9.

37. Blomberg and Robinson, *How Wide the Divide?* 20.

Chapter 5: Continual Revelation and Mormon Scriptural Books

1. Craig L. Blomberg and Stephen E. Robinson, *How Wide the Divide? A Mormon & an Evangelical in Conversation* (Downers Grove, IL: InterVarsity Press, 1997), 57.

2. Ibid., 58. As Brigham Young University scholar Dr. Stephen Robinson affirms, "The record of revelation cannot logically be more authoritative than the experience of revelation."

3. The Mormons believe that the LDS President speaks sometimes as Prophet, and sometimes as merely expressing his own opinions. See Stephen E. Robinson, *Are Mormons Christians?* (Salt Lake City: Bookcraft, 1991), 15.

4. *Doctrine and Covenants* (hereafter *DC*) 28:2–7.

5. Blomberg and Robinson, *How Wide the Divide?* 59.

6. *DC* 8; LDS Church Educational System, *Doctrine and Covenants: Student Manual, Religion 324 and 325* (Salt Lake City: The Church of Jesus Christ of Latter-day Saints, 1981), 18–19.

7. Blomberg and Robinson, *How Wide the Divide?* 15.

8. Ibid., 140.

9. *DC* 134:10. LDS Church excommunication is a disciplinary process used only in extreme situations. This includes removal of an individual's name from the records of the church. Excommunicated individuals have the opportunity to return and have their church membership restored through the process of repentance and baptism by immersion for the remission of sins.

10. Bruce McConkie's theological influence on the LDS Church is unprecedented; his book *Mormon Doctrine* is the all-time LDS best seller.

11. Blomberg and Robinson, *How Wide the Divide?* 55.

12. Christians use several descriptive theological words to explain their position and absolute belief concerning the total uniqueness and authority of the Bible. The primary descriptive terms are *inerrancy*, *infallibility*, *verbal inspiration*, and *plenary inspiration*. *Verbal* means that the process of inspiration extends to the actual words of the Bible, not just the thoughts and concepts embraced in them. *Plenary* means that all sixty-six books in all their parts are inspired. It precludes an appeal to a "canon within the canon," that is, to treating only parts of the Bible as inspired, trustworthy, or authoritative. Mormons reject this regular evangelical theological terminology because the exact words are not found in the Bible.

See Blomberg and Robinson, *How Wide the Divide?* 20n5. Mormons do not believe in the verbal and plenary inspiration, inerrancy, sufficiency, and trustworthiness of the Bible, nor do they maintain a closed-canon view of Scripture.

13. See *Doctrine and Covenants Student Manual*, 40.

14. Bruce R. McConkie, *Mormon Doctrine*, 2d ed. (Salt Lake City: Bookcraft, 1966), 455.

15. Blomberg and Robinson, *How Wide the Divide?* 33.

16. Robert L. Millet, *A Different Jesus? The Christ of the Latter-day Saints* (Grand Rapids, MI: Eerdmans, 2005), 61.

17. Blomberg and Robinson, *How Wide the Divide?* 56.

18. Ibid.

19. *Book of Mormon*: 1 Nephi 13:25–27; LDS Church Educational System, *Church History in the Fulness of Times, Religion 341–43* (Salt Lake City: The Church of Jesus Christ of Latter-day Saints, 1993), 83.

20. Blomberg and Robinson, *How Wide the Divide?* 63.

21. 1 Nephi 13:28, 39; LDS Church Educational System, *Book of Mormon: Student Manual, Religion 121 and 122* (Salt Lake City: The Church of Jesus Christ of Latter-day Saints, 1996), 14.

22. Blomberg and Robinson, *How Wide the Divide?* 63.

23. McConkie, *Mormon Doctrine*, 453–55.

24. 1 Nephi 13:25–29; DC 73, 76; *Doctrine and Covenants Student Manual*, 153–54, 158.

25. DC 73; *Doctrine and Covenants Student Manual*, 153.

26. DC 73; *Doctrine and Covenants Student Manual*, 154.

27. DC 43; *Doctrine and Covenants Student Manual*, 88.

28. *Book of Mormon Student Manual*, 14; Blomberg and Robinson, *How Wide the Divide?* 51.

29. Blomberg and Robinson, *How Wide the Divide?* 200n11.

30. Ibid., 36.

31. Millet, *A Different Jesus?* 60.

32. Blomberg and Robinson, *How Wide the Divide?* 56.

33. Rex E. Lee, *What Do Mormons Believe?* (Salt Lake City: Deseret, 1992), 16; DC 20:9; 42:12.

34. *Book of Mormon Student Manual*, 1. Mormon theologian Bruce McConkie makes this even clearer: "Almost all of the doctrines of the gospel are taught in the *Book of Mormon* with much greater clarity and perfection than those same doctrines are revealed in the Bible. Anyone who will place in parallel columns the teachings of these two great books on such subjects as the atonement, plan of salvation, gathering of Israel, baptism, gifts of the Spirit, miracles, revelation, faith, charity—or any of a hundred other subjects—will find conclusive proof of the superiority of *Book of Mormon* teachings." McConkie, *Mormon Doctrine*, 99.

35. *Book of Mormon*: Ether.

36. *Book of Mormon Student Manual*, 16.

37. Lee, *What Do Mormons Believe?* 14.

38. 1 Nephi 2:20; *Book of Mormon Student Manual*, 17.

39. *Book of Mormon*: 2 Nephi 5:15.

40. Ibid., 5:21.

41. *Book of Mormon*: Mormon 6.

42. McConkie, *Mormon Doctrine*, 32–33; Richard and Joan Ostling, *Mormon America: The Power and the Promise* (New York: HarperSanFrancisco, 1999), 273.

43. Mormon 8:3; 9:24.

44. *Book of Mormon*: 3 Nephi 11–28; Lee, *What Do Mormons Believe?* 17.

45. Ostling and Ostling, *Mormon America*, 259.

46. DC 9:8–9.

47. *Book of Mormon Student Manual*, v; DC 9; *Doctrine and Covenants Student Manual*, 21.

48. Ostling and Ostling, *Mormon America*, chap. 16.

49. Smithsonian Institution, *Statement Regarding the Book of Mormon* (Spring 1986).

50. Francis J. Beckwith, Carl Mosser, and Paul Owen, eds., *The New Mormon Challenge: Responding to the Latest Defenses of a Fast-Growing Movement* (Grand Rapids, MI: Zondervan, 2002), chap. 10.

51. Blomberg and Robinson, *How Wide the Divide?* 48–50.

52. *Doctrine and Covenants Student Manual*, vii.

53. Ibid., vii, 2.

54. Ibid., 1–2.

55. The name *Pearl of Great Price* is taken from Jesus' parable found in Matthew 13:45–46.

56. Joseph Smith, *History of the Church*, 1:98–101, 131–39.

57. Ibid., 4:519–34.

58. Ostling and Ostling, *Mormon America*, 281.

59. Ibid., 282.

60. See "The Lost Book of Abraham," www.bookofabraham.info.

61. Smith, *History of the Church*, 1:1–44.

62. Ibid., 4:535–41.

Chapter 6: The Worldview of Mormonism

1. Francis J. Beckwith, Carl Mosser, and Paul Owen, eds., *The New Mormon Challenge: Responding to the Latest Defenses of a Fast-Growing Movement* (Grand Rapids, MI: Zondervan, 2002), 90–267.

2. Robert Millet, *A Different Jesus? The Christ of the Latter-day Saints* (Grand Rapids, MI: Eerdmans, 2005), 182.

3. Craig Blomberg and Stephen Robinson, *How Wide the Divide? A Mormon & an Evangelical in Conversation* (Downers Grove, IL: InterVarsity Press, 1997), 18.

4. James W. Sire, *The Universe Next Door: A Basic Worldview Catalog* (Downers Grove, IL: InterVarsity Press, 1988), 16–20.

5. Ibid., 18.

6. www.lds.org. See under "About the Church: Basic Beliefs."

7. Beckwith, Mosser, and Owen, *New Mormon Challenge*, 190–91; see also Millet, *A Different Jesus?* 25–27.

8. *Primordial* means "having to do with the prime order of things, the origins, the first to begin, the first created or developed, things that exist in or persist from the beginning."

9. Beckwith, Mosser, and Owen, *New Mormon Challenge*, 179–86.

10. Ibid., 159–64.

11. *Doctrine and Covenants* (hereafter *DC*) 88:13.

12. Joseph Fielding Smith, *Doctrines of Salvation* (Salt Lake City: Cannon and Sons, 1891), 37; Beckwith, Mosser, and Owen, *New Mormon Challenge*, 168, 182.

13. Bruce R. McConkie, *Mormon Doctrine*, 2d ed. (Salt Lake City: Bookcraft, 1966), 386–87, 751.

14. *DC* 93:29–30; see also *DC* 93:36; LDS Church Educational System, *Doctrine and Covenants: Student Manual, Religion 324 and 325* (Salt Lake City: The Church of Jesus Christ of Latter-day Saints, 1981), 219.

15. Joseph Smith, "King Follett Sermon," in *History of the Church*, 6:302–317. There is apparently some debate among Mormons over how synonymously Joseph Smith thought of "intelligences" and "spirits" and over the details of "spirit-birth," which some Mormons believe started with Brigham Young.

16. Beckwith, Mosser, and Owen, *New Mormon Challenge*, 181.

17. Many Mormons do not usually identify the spirit and soul as synonymous, although some do. Often Mormons define the soul as the united entity of the spirit with the physical body. *DC* 88:15–16.

18. *Pearl of Great Price*: Abraham 3:22–23; *DC* 93:29; *Doctrine and Covenants Student Manual*, 220.

19. *DC* 93:29–30; *Doctrine and Covenants Student Manual*, 219.

20. DC 131:1; LDS Church Educational System, *Church History in the Fulness of Times, Religion 341–43* (Salt Lake City: The Church of Jesus Christ of Latter-day Saints, 1993), 326.

21. See also *Doctrine and Covenants Student Manual*, 326.

22. *Church History in the Fulness of Times*, 326.

23. DC 88:37; *Doctrine and Covenants Student Manual*, 200.

24. Brigham Young, *Journal of Discourses*, 7:333. www.journalofdiscourses.org.

25. Ibid., 14:71–72.

26. McConkie, *Mormon Doctrine*, 131, 163, 576–77, 579.

27. *Encyclopedia of Mormonism*, s.v. "Creation" (New York: Macmillan, 1992), 340.

28. McConkie, *Mormon Doctrine*, 164–66.

29. Blomberg and Robinson, *How Wide the Divide?* 85, 87. Stephen Robinson states that Smith's "King Follett" discourse is quasi-official in the LDS Church; *Encyclopedia of Mormonism*, s.v. "Creation," 340–43.

30. Smith, "King Follett Sermon," in *History of the Church*, 6:302–317.

31. Young, *Journal of Discourses*, 14:116, www.journalofdiscourses.org.

32. Abraham 4:1.

33. Beckwith, Mosser, and Owen, *New Mormon Challenge*, 164, 168–70.

34. Richard R. Hopkins, *Biblical Mormonism: Responding to Evangelical Criticism of LDS Theology* (Bountiful, UT: Horizon, 1994), 102.

35. Abraham 3:2–4; 5:13.

36. Blomberg and Robinson, *How Wide the Divide?* 18.

37. McConkie, *Mormon Doctrine*, 38.

38. *Encyclopedia of Mormonism*, s.v. "Animals," 42.

39. *Book of Mormon*: Moses 3:5; 6:5.

40. God the Father is the Father of spirits (Heb. 12:9).

41. Blomberg and Robinson, *How Wide the Divide?* 18.

42. McConkie, *Mormon Doctrine*, 84.

43. Ibid., 516.

44. Ibid., 751.

45. Ibid., 84–85.

46. Ibid., 589–90.

47. Robert Millet, *The Mormon Faith: A New Look at Christianity* (Salt Lake City: Shadow Mountain, 1998), 56–56.

48. Wayne Grudem, *Bible Doctrine: Essential Teachings of the Christian Faith* (Grand Rapids, MI: Zondervan, 1999), 168–74.

49. Millet, *Mormon Faith*, 38–42, 114–17; McConkie, *Mormon Doctrine*, 35–37.

50. Parley P. Pratt, *Key to the Science of Theology* (Salt Lake City: Deseret, 1978), 21.

51. Hopkins, *Biblical Mormonism*, 101.

52. Millet, *Mormon Faith*, 40.

53. DC 132:16–17; *Encyclopedia of Mormonism*, s.v. "Angels," 40–42.

54. www.lds.org. See under "A–Z Index: Agency."

55. Blomberg and Robinson, *How Wide the Divide?* 146.

56. The teaching of a monk named Pelagius in the fifth century AD. He taught that man's will was and still is free to choose good or evil, and that there is no inherited sin (through Adam). He taught that every infant born into the world is in the same condition as Adam before the fall and becomes a sinner because he sins.

57. LDS Church Educational System, *Book of Mormon: Student Manual, Religion 121 and 122* (Salt Lake City: The Church of Jesus Christ of Latter-day Saints, 1996), 56.

58. Joseph Fielding Smith Jr., *Doctrines of Salvation: Sermons and Writings of Joseph Fielding Smith*, 3 vols. (Salt Lake City: Deseret, 1957–1963), 1:61.

59. John J. Steward and William E. Bennett, *Mormonism and the Negro* (Orem, UT: Community Press, 1960), 46–47.

60. McConkie, *Mormon Doctrine*, 114.

61. Ibid., 616.

62. *Book of Mormon*: Alma 24:14; Moses 6:62.

63. Alma 42:8.

64. *Book of Mormon*: Jacob 6:8; Alma 12:30.

65. Moses 4:3.

66. Moses 4:2; Abraham 3:27.

67. Mormons believe this family war is described in Revelation 12:9–12.

68. Moses 4:4; Abraham 3:27–28; Young, *Journal of Discourses*, 5:331, www.journalofdiscourses.org.

69. Millet, *Mormon Faith*, 32.

70. Millet, *A Different Jesus?* 196.

71. Stephen E. Robinson, *Are Mormons Christians?* (Salt Lake City: Bookcraft, 1991), 19–20; Blomberg and Robinson, *How Wide the Divide?* 106.

72. McConkie, *Mormon Doctrine*, 18.

73. www.mormonwiki.org/purposeoflife.

74. www.Mormon.org.

75. Joseph Fielding Smith Jr., *Doctrines of Salvation*, 1:69–70.

76. Brigham Young, *Discourses of Brigham Young*, comp. John A. Widtoe (Salt Lake City: Deseret, 1978), 197.

Chapter 7: Gods and the Mormon Gospel of Deification

1. *Doctrine and Covenants* (hereafter DC) 132:20; Joseph Smith, "King Follett Sermon," in *History of the Church*, 6:302–17; Stephen E. Robinson, *Are Mormons Christians?* (Salt Lake City: Bookcraft, 1991), 60, 91.

2. President Snow often referred to this couplet as having been revealed to him by inspiration during the Nauvoo, Illinois, period of the Mormon Church (*Deseret Weekly* 49, November 1894, 610). Many non-Mormons make the mistake either of believing that all Mormons believe in the entire Lorenzo Snow couplet or of over-generalizing that Mormonism has fully abandoned it. It is important that we do not embrace either stereotype. Within Mormonism today there seems to be a diversity of opinions and positions related to the Lorenzo Snow couplet.

3. *Encyclopedia of Mormonism*, s.v. "Christology" (New York: Macmillan, 1992), 273.

4. Richard and Joan Ostling, *Mormon America: The Power and the Promise* (New York: HarperSanFrancisco, 1999), 305–7; DC 121:32; *Pearl of Great Price*: Abraham 4:1.

5. Bruce R. McConkie, *Mormon Doctrine*, 2d ed. (Salt Lake City: Bookcraft, 1966), 576–77.

6. Ibid., 579.

7. Francis J. Beckwith, Carl Mosser, and Paul Owen, eds., *The New Mormon Challenge: Responding to the Latest Defenses of a Fast-Growing Movement* (Grand Rapids, MI: Zondervan, 2002), 198.

8. Craig Blomberg and Stephen Robinson, *How Wide the Divide? A Mormon & an Evangelical in Conversation* (Downers Grove, IL: InterVarsity Press, 1997), 111n2, 141.

9. Robert L. Millet, *A Different Jesus? The Christ of the Latter-day Saints* (Grand Rapids, MI: Eerdmans, 2005), 141; Blomberg and Robinson, *How Wide the Divide?* 129, 131.

10. Robinson, *Are Mormons Christians?* 72.

11. DC 130:22.

12. McConkie, *Mormon Doctrine*, 576.

13. Ibid., 319.

14. Blomberg and Robinson, *How Wide the Divide?* 78.

15. Ibid., 116.

16. *Book of Mormon*: 2 Nephi 31:7, 12; 3 Nephi 28:11.

17. Blomberg and Robinson, *How Wide the Divide?* 131.

18. Robert Millet, *The Mormon Faith: A New Look at Christianity* (Salt Lake City: Shadow Mountain, 1998), 29.

19. McConkie, *Mormon Doctrine*, 322.

20. Ibid., 319.

21. Ibid., 322.

22. Blomberg and Robinson, *How Wide the Divide?* 117.

23. Ibid., 89–92.

24. *Pearl of Great Price*: Moses 6:57; McConkie, *Mormon Doctrine*, 467.

25. Blomberg and Robinson, *How Wide the Divide?* 78; Moses 6:57; DC 130:22.

26. Blomberg and Robinson, *How Wide the Divide?* 80.

27. LDS Church Educational System, *Doctrines of the Gospel: Student Manual, Religion 231 and 232* (Salt Lake City: The Church of Jesus Christ of Latter-day Saints, 1986), 8.

28. McConkie, *Mormon Doctrine*, 258, 751.

29. *Doctrines of the Gospel Student Manual*, 7.

30. Millet, *A Different Jesus?* 144.

31. Smith, "King Follett Sermon," in *History of the Church*, 6:302–317.

32. Millet, *Mormon Faith*, 29.

33. DC 93:21; Blomberg and Robinson, *How Wide the Divide?* 78.

34. McConkie, *Mormon Doctrine*, 129. See also 323.

35. 3 Nephi 9:15; *Book of Mormon*: Helaman 14:12; Moses 1:33; DC 93:10.

36. *Doctrines of the Gospel Student Manual*, 11.

37. Mormons attempt to argue that because Jesus Christ became a human in his incarnation, then it is only logical to believe that humans can also become gods. Using the unique case study of the incarnation of Jesus Christ, Mormons argue that if the divine can become fully human, then humans can become fully gods (see Phil. 2:6–11).

38. Blomberg and Robinson, *How Wide the Divide?* 83–84. Dr. Robinson admits that the LDS view of deification is based on only three passages from LDS scriptures: DC 76:58; 121:28, 32; 132.

39. Millet, *A Different Jesus?* 117. Although fully embracing the Mormon doctrine of human deification, Brigham Young University scholars such as Stephen Robinson and Robert Millet emphasize that we cannot fully understand or comprehend the details and activities of human exaltation and deification.

40. *Encyclopedia of Mormonism*, s.v. "Christology," 273.

41. Blomberg and Robinson, *How Wide the Divide?* 209n11, 18.

42. Millet, *A Different Jesus?* 144.

43. Blomberg and Robinson, *How Wide the Divide?* 18.

44. *Encyclopedia of Mormonism*, s.v. "Christology," 272–73.

45. Millet, *A Different Jesus?* 83; Abraham 3:22–23; DC 93:29.

46. DC 93:29–30.

47. Blomberg and Robinson, *How Wide the Divide?* 79.

48. Beckwith, Mosser, and Owen, *New Mormon Challenge*, 79, 82.

49. Blomberg and Robinson, *How Wide the Divide?* 82–83.

50. Ibid., 91, 95–96.

51. The most helpful categorizations of God's unique characteristics and attributes are found in the theological distinction that Protestant Reformers have made between the *communicable* and *incommunicable* attributes of God. For a thorough explanation of God's attributes, see Wayne Grudem, *Bible Doctrine: Essential Teachings of the Christian Faith* (Grand Rapids, MI: Zondervan, 1999), 67–102.

52. Blomberg and Robinson, *How Wide the Divide?* 82. See also 86–87, 91. Although in my view Mormons are somewhat contradictory in their own writings, Dr. Craig Blomberg told me that many informed Mormons would unequivocally say that their understanding of deification means that one day we will share perfectly God's communicable attributes only. They do not claim we will ever be omnipotent, omniscient, or omnipresent. They stress that we will always be dependent on and contingent on God. We will never become beings that anyone else worships. All worship for all eternity will be reserved for God, through Christ, in the power of the Holy Ghost. We must ask, then,

why spirit-children of the Father worship Jesus and the Holy Spirit, who are themselves other spirit-children who progressed into gods. If it occurs today, why wouldn't it logically occur in the future?

53. Blomberg and Robinson, *How Wide the Divide?* 83.

54. Ibid., 92.

55. Ibid., 80; Millet, *A Different Jesus?* 116.

56. Those interested in the real deification teaching of early Christians may wish to read Timothy Ware, *The Orthodox Church* (London: Penguin, 1997).

57. Grudem, *Bible Doctrine*, 356–58.

58. Blomberg and Robinson, *How Wide the Divide?* 101.

59. Ibid., 107.

Chapter 8: The Heavens and Hell of Mormonism

1. Although Mormonism does not specifically use the phrase *partial salvation*, it accurately describes what Mormons mean by the state of occupants of kingdoms of lesser glory who lack the fullness of salvation.

2. Bruce McConkie, *Mormon Doctrine*, 2d ed. (Salt Lake City: Bookcraft, 1966), 669–73; Robert L. Millet, *A Different Jesus? The Christ of the Latter-day Saints* (Grand Rapids, MI: Eerdmans, 2005), 94.

3. Rom. 1:16–17.

4. Millet, *A Different Jesus?* 108–9.

5. *Book of Mormon*: Alma 40:4; 11:41–44; *Doctrine and Covenants* (hereafter *DC*) 29:26.

6. *Pearl of Great Price*: Moses 1:39 reads: "This is my work and my glory—to bring to pass the immortality and eternal life of man"; see Robert Millet, *The Mormon Faith: A New Look at Christianity* (Salt Lake City: Shadow Mountain, 1998), 52.

7. McConkie, *Mormon Doctrine*, 669, 671.

8. LDS Church Educational System, *Doctrine and Covenants: Student Manual, Religion 324–325* (Salt Lake City: The Church of Jesus Christ of Latter-day Saints, 1981), 355.

9. Ibid.

10. Robert Millet, *Mormon Faith*, 52.

11. www.lds.org. See under "A–Z Index: Eternal Life."; see also *DC* 131:1–4; *Doctrine and Covenants Student Manual*, 355.

12. Millet, *A Different Jesus?* 115.

13. Craig Blomberg and Stephen Robinson, *How Wide the Divide? A Mormon & an Evangelical in Conversation* (Downers Grove, IL: InterVarsity Press, 1997), 18.

14. *Doctrine and Covenants Student Manual*, 338.

15. Ibid., 358.

16. Ibid., 60.

17. Ibid., 258.

18. LDS Church Educational System, *Book of Mormon: Student Manual, Religion 121 and 122* (Salt Lake City: The Church of Jesus Christ of Latter-day Saints, 1996), 36.

19. Ibid.; *Doctrine and Covenants Student Manual*, 333, 358.

20. *DC* 137:10; *Doctrine and Covenants Student Manual*, 355–56. "We were all mature spirits before we were born, and the bodies of little children will grow after the resurrection to the full stature of the spirit, and all the blessings will be theirs through their obedience, the same as if they had lived to maturity and received them on the earth."

21. See Blomberg and Robinson, *How Wide the Divide?* 133–34, 153–54. "Latter-day Saints do not derive their belief in the three degrees of glory (heaven) primarily from the Bible. . . . It comes from modern revelation. . . ."

22. Richard Lyman Bushman, *Joseph Smith: Rough Stone Rolling: A Cultural Biography of Mormonism's Founder* (New York: Vintage Books, 2005), 195–214.

23. *DC* 76:11–14, 18–19 reads: "We, Joseph Smith, Jr., and Sidney Rigdon, being in the Spirit on the sixteenth day of February, in the year of our Lord one thousand eight hundred and thirty-two—By the

power of the Spirit our eyes were opened and our understandings were enlightened, so as to see and understand the things of God. Even those things which were from the beginning before the world was, which were ordained of the Father, through his Only Begotten Son, who was in the bosom of the Father, even from the beginning; Of whom we bear record; and the record which we bear is the fulness of the gospel of Jesus Christ, who is the Son, whom we saw and with whom we conversed in the heavenly vision. . . . Now this caused us to marvel, for it was given unto us of the Spirit. And while we meditated upon these things, the Lord touched the eyes of our understandings and they were opened, and the glory of the Lord shone round about."

24. *DC* 76:15–17.

25. Blomberg and Robinson, *How Wide the Divide?* 151. Though some Mormons believe that a person can still progress within the permanent kingdom they have been assigned by God.

26. Ibid., 152.

27. *Doctrine and Covenants Student Manual*, 325.

28. Richard and Joan Ostling, *Mormon America: The Power and the Promise* (New York: HarperSanFrancisco, 1999), 167. No proxy temple marriages are performed for the dead, although some Mormons apparently state that this might change during the millennium. *Doctrine and Covenants Student Manual*, sec. 132.

29. *Doctrine and Covenants Student Manual*, 164, 445; Blomberg and Robinson, *How Wide the Divide?* 150, 153; *DC* 137:7; McConkie, *Mormon Doctrine*, 686; Millet, *A Different Jesus?* chap. 6.

30. *DC* 132:16–17; *Doctrine and Covenants Student Manual*, 327–28.

31. *DC* 76:71–80.

32. *Doctrine and Covenants Student Manual*, 164, 446; *DC* 76:71–78; Blomberg and Robinson, *How Wide the Divide?* 152.

33. Coke Newell, *Latter Days: A Guided Tour through Six Billion Years of Mormonism* (New York: St. Martin's Press, 2000), 242.

34. *DC* 76:81–85; *Doctrine and Covenants Student Manual*, 165–66. "After their resurrection, the great majority of those who have suffered in hell (spirit-prison) will pass into the Telestial kingdom."

35. Mark 9:47–48; Rev. 20:14–15.

36. Millet, *A Different Jesus?* 205.

37. Rev. 20:12–14.

38. Blomberg and Robinson, *How Wide the Divide?* 173–74; see also Craig Blomberg, "Degrees of Reward in the Kingdom of Heaven?" *Journal of the Evangelical Theological Society* 35 (1992): 159–72.

Chapter 9: Jesus, Plus Much More

1. When Joseph Smith emphasized that "all mankind *may* be saved," he was making a statement against Calvinism's teaching concerning predestination or election, that men or women are decreed by God to salvation or reprobation. This does not mean, however, that the LDS Church believes that all humankind *will* be saved.

2. *Book of Mormon*: 2 Nephi 25:23 reads, "For we know that it is by grace that we are saved, after all we can do."

3. Robert Millet, *The Mormon Faith: A New Look at Christianity* (Salt Lake City: Shadow Mountain, 1998), 69.

4. www.lds.org. See under "A–Z Index: Ordinances"; see also Robert Millet, *A Different Jesus? The Christ of the Latter-day Saints* (Grand Rapids, MI: Eerdmans, 2005), 201.

5. Robert Millet, *Grace Works* (Salt Lake City: Deseret, 2003), 117.

6. Millet, *A Different Jesus?* 59; Richard and Joan Ostling, *Mormon America: The Power and the Promise* (New York: HarperSanFrancisco, 1999), chap. 12.

7. Bruce R. McConkie, *Mormon Doctrine*, 2d ed. (Salt Lake City: Bookcraft, 1966), 669–72.

8. Millet, *A Different Jesus?* 194; Richard R. Hopkins, *Biblical Mormonism: Respond-*

ing to Evangelical Criticism of LDS Theology (Bountiful, UT: Horizon, 1994), 12, 14.

9. LDS Church Educational System, *Book of Mormon: Student Manual, Religion 121 and 122* (Salt Lake City: The Church of Jesus Christ of Latter-day Saints, 1996), 36; see also 2 Nephi 25:23.

10. McConkie, *Mormon Doctrine*, 671.

11. Ibid., 95.

12. Craig Blomberg and Stephen Robinson, *How Wide the Divide? A Mormon & an Evangelical in Conversation* (Downers Grove, IL: InterVarsity Press, 1997), 145–46.

13. Ibid., 73.

14. Stephen E. Robinson, *Believing Christ* (Salt Lake City: Deseret, 1992), 45.

15. Rom. 1:16.

16. McConkie, *Mormon Doctrine*, 208; see also LDS Church Educational System, *Doctrine and Covenants: Student Manual, Religion 324 and 325* (Salt Lake City: The Church of Jesus Christ of Latter-day Saints, 1981), 41.

17. John Piper, *Counted Righteous in Christ: Should We Abandon the Imputation of Christ's Righteousness?* (Wheaton, IL: Crossway, 2002), 41. Imputation is the act in which God counts sinners to be righteous through their faith in Christ on the basis of Christ's perfect "blood and righteousness," specifically the righteousness that Christ accomplished by his perfect obedience in life and death.

18. Ibid., 58, 89, 122. See Rom. 10:4; 2 Cor. 5:21; Phil. 3:9.

19. Piper, *Counted Righteous*, 89.

20. Stephen E. Robinson, *Are Mormons Christians?* (Salt Lake City: Bookcraft, 1991), 106. Mormons emphasize that LDS covenant obligations are required for eternal salvation. "We participate in our own salvation as we attempt to keep the commandments of God, but we can never earn it ourselves or bring it to pass on our own merits" (106). No matter how it is said, however, the degree to which Mormons are obedient to what they call covenant obliga-

tions has a direct correlation to the degree of glory with which they will be rewarded in eternity. Eternal salvation is conditional on whether one puts his or her total faith in Christ or not.

21. Piper, *Counted Righteous*, 122.

22. Wayne Grudem, *Bible Doctrine: Essential Teachings of the Christian Faith* (Grand Rapids, MI: Zondervan, 1999), 316, 326.

23. Millet, *A Different Jesus?* 98–102. Robert Millet seems to present a more biblical view of justification and sanctification. He still emphasizes, however, that justification in Christ is received and secured only through water baptism and the confirmation sacrament in only the Mormon Church, through its male priesthoods.

24. Blomberg and Robinson, *How Wide the Divide?* 168–69.

25. www.lds.org. See under "A–Z Index: Repentance."

26. Millet, *A Different Jesus?* 49, 92; *Book of Mormon*: Mosiah 3:7. Mormons believe that the atonement of Christ began in the garden of Gethsemane and was completed on the cross.

27. www.lds.org. See under "A–Z Index: Atonement of Jesus Christ."

28. Thorough studies of water baptism in the New Testament are available in G. R. Beasley-Murray, *Baptism in the New Testament* (Grand Rapids, MI: Eerdmans, 1962), and Paul K. Jewett, *Infant Baptism and the Covenant of Grace* (Grand Rapids, MI: Eerdmans, 1978).

29. Mormons do not believe in infant baptism.

30. Rex E. Lee, *What Do Mormons Believe?* (Salt Lake City: Deseret, 1992), 42–43.

31. *Doctrine and Covenants* (hereafter *DC*) 68:27.

32. *Encyclopedia of Mormonism*, s.v. "Baptismal Prayer" (New York: Macmillan, 1992), 95.

33. Mormons must still merit the constant companionship of the Holy Spirit.

34. Clark L. and Kathryn H. Kidd, *A Convert's Guide to Mormon Life: A Guidebook for New Members of the Church of Jesus Christ of Latter-day Saints* (Salt Lake City: Bookcraft, 1998), 250.

35. www.lds.org. See under "A–Z Index: Temples."

36. Robinson, *Are Mormons Christians?* 109.

37. The Second Temple in Jerusalem was destroyed by the Romans in AD 70.

38. Ostling and Ostling, *Mormon America*, 188, 194.

39. The LDS Church opens a temple for visits by non-Mormons shortly after its construction and before the official dedication by the general church authorities and also after a temple renovation.

40. *Doctrine and Covenants Student Manual*, 207.

41. Ostling and Ostling, *Mormon America*, 186.

42. Robinson, *Are Mormons Christians?* 97. To provide New Testament backing for secret Mormon temple ordinances, Stephen Robinson points to 1 Corinthians 2:6–7 and 2 Corinthians 12:4 to emphasize that Paul taught a secret wisdom to the mature and initiated.

43. Ibid., 96.

44. Ostling and Ostling, *Mormon America*, 193.

45. Ibid., 180–81.

46. *Doctrine and Covenants Student Manual*, 327–28, 333, 358.

47. Ostling and Ostling, *Mormon America*, 167.

48. Lee, *What Do Mormons Believe?* 32.

49. DC 119; *Doctrine and Covenants Student Manual*, 292.

50. DC 119:5–6; *Doctrine and Covenants Student Manual*, 294.

51. Ostling and Ostling, *Mormon America*, 178–79.

52. *Doctrine and Covenants Student Manual*, 207.

53. Ibid., 206.

Chapter 10: How the Dead Are Saved in Mormonism

1. F. F. Bruce, *The New International Commentary on the New Testament: The Epistle of Hebrews* (Grand Rapids, MI: Eerdmans, 1964), 222; Donald Guthrie, *Tyndale New Testament Commentaries: Hebrews* (Grand Rapids, MI: Eerdmans, 1988), 199; J. I. Packer, "Can the Dead Be Converted?" *Christianity Today*, January 11, 1999. As Packer emphasizes, when the writer of Hebrews uses the word *once*, he means "once and for all," and no second salvation opportunities follow human death.

2. LDS Church Educational System, *Doctrine and Covenants: Student Manual, Religion 324 and 325* (Salt Lake City: The Church of Jesus Christ of Latter-day Saints, 1981), Enrichment O, 445–49.

3. Joseph Smith, *History of the Church*, 6:313.

4. *Doctrine and Covenants Student Manual*, 6–8; Bruce R. McConkie, *Mormon Doctrine*, 2d ed. (Salt Lake City: Bookcraft, 1966), 223; *Doctrine and Covenants* (hereafter DC) 76:103–6.

5. DC 2:2.

6. Matt. 17:1–13.

7. DC 110:13–16.

8. Ibid., 2:1–13; 110:13–16.

9. McConkie, *Mormon Doctrine*, 683.

10. *Doctrine and Covenants Student Manual*, 445.

11. Ibid., 445.

12. McConkie, *Mormon Doctrine*, 762.

13. www.lds.org—*True to the Faith*, 111. Joseph Smith stated that the passage in which Jesus was on the cross and told the thief next to him that today he would be with him in paradise was mistranslated. Smith stated that instead of "paradise," it should read "the world of spirits."

14. Ibid.

15. DC 138:2; *Book of Mormon*: Alma 11–14. Latter-day Saints believe that when Jesus declared in Matthew 16:18, "I tell you, you are Peter, and on this rock I will

build my church, and the gates of hell shall not prevail against it," he was referring to spirit-prison.

16. *DC* 138:30–35.

17. Ibid., 76:36–37; Alma 12:16–18.

18. McConkie, *Mormon Doctrine*, 349; see also *DC* 76:103–6.

19. Alma 40:13–14; *Book of Mormon*: 2 Nephi 9:6–12.

20. *DC* 138; Robert L. Millet, *A Different Jesus? The Christ of the Latter-day Saints* (Grand Rapids, MI: Eerdmans, 2005), 135.

21. Latter-day Saints emphasize that this immense gulf between Mormon paradise and those suffering in spirit-prison is described in Jesus' parable of the rich man and Lazarus (Luke 16:19–31).

22. Alma 40:11–15; McConkie, *Mormon Doctrine*, 755; *DC* 124:130.

23. *Encyclopedia of Mormonism*, "Jesus," www.lib.byu.edu/MacMillan.

24. Brigham Young, *Journal of Discourses*, 4:285.

25. Millet, *A Different Jesus?* 136.

26. *Doctrine and Covenants Student Manual*, 445.

27. Ibid., 446.

28. McConkie, *Mormon Doctrine*, 685–87.

29. Ibid., 685.

30. Ibid., 686.

31. Ibid.

32. Millet, *A Different Jesus?* chap. 6.

33. Blomberg and Robinson, *How Wide the Divide?* 149.

34. Ibid., 150.

35. Millet, *A Different Jesus?* 135.

36. *Encyclopedia of Mormonism*, "Temple Ordinances," www.lib.byu.edu/MacMillan.

37. *Doctrine and Covenants Student Manual*, 446.

38. Clark and Kathryn Kidd, *A Convert's Guide to Mormon Life: A Guidebook for New Members of the Church of Jesus Christ of Latter-day Saints* (Salt Lake City: Bookcraft, 1998), 195.

39. *Doctrine and Covenants Student Manual*, 447–48.

40. *Encyclopedia of Mormonism*, "Baptism for the Dead," www.lib.byu.edu/MacMillan.

41. *Doctrine and Covenants Student Manual*, 314.

42. See D. A. Carson, "Did Paul Baptize for the Dead?" *Christianity Today*, August 10, 1998. When something is mentioned only once in the Bible, misusing or misinterpreting it is very easy. One Bible verse should never be seen as carrying the same theological weight of the primary themes found throughout the Bible. Unfortunately, this is exactly what Mormonism has done here.

43. Craig Blomberg, *The NIV Application Commentary: 1 Corinthians* (Grand Rapids, MI: Zondervan, 1994), 299. Early church fathers allude to such a practice among second-century gnostic groups, in which living believers were baptized on behalf of those in their sect who had died without being baptized. Given the Corinthians' tendencies toward early gnostic belief and practice, it is not difficult to imagine something similar having begun among at least a few in Corinth.

44. McConkie, *Mormon Doctrine*, 501.

45. See Rev. 20:4; *DC* 29:11.

46. McConkie, *Mormon Doctrine*, 29; Robert Millet, *The Mormon Faith: A New Look at Christianity* (Salt Lake City: Shadow Mountain, 1998), 159; *DC* 101:23–31.

47. LDS Church Educational System, *Doctrines of the Gospel: Student Manual, Religion 231 and 232* (Salt Lake City: The Church of Jesus Christ of Latter-day Saints, 1986), 104; *Book of Mormon*: 3 Nephi 20:22; 21:20–29; *Book of Mormon*: Ether 13:1–12.

48. *DC* 88:111–15; Millet, *Mormon Faith*, 161.

49. McConkie, *Mormon Doctrine*, 51; *DC* 29:22–25; Millet, *Mormon Faith*, 162.

index of names

Aaron, 28
Abraham, 41–42, 74, 89, 90–91, 117
Adam, 90, 104, 106, 107–8, 116, 117, 172, 178, 182
Adams, Jim, 94
Alger, Fanny, 40

Benson, Ezra Taft, 84
Blomberg, Craig, 14, 75, 83, 88, 135, 142, 163, 200n52
Brunson, Seymour, 169
Buchanan, James, 56
Bullard, Isaac, 190n6
Burgess, 43
Bushman, Richard Lyman, 13, 21, 27

Cain, 105
Calvin, John, 70
Campbell, Alexander, 35
Cowdery, Oliver, 26, 27, 28–29, 30, 34, 41, 42, 75, 159, 178, 192n49
Cumming, Alfred, 56

Dow, Lorenzo, 190n6

Elijah, 19, 29, 42–43, 159
Elohim, 113, 115
Enoch, 33, 90
Eve, 106, 107–8, 117, 182

Fillmore, Millard, 56

Finney, Charles, 190n6
Follett, King, 48, 95, 98

Gabriel (angel), 104
Gilbert, John, 29
Grandin, Egert, 29
Grudem, Wayne, 141

Hale, Emma. *See* Smith, Emma
Hale, Isaac, 25, 33
Handel, George Frideric, 27
Harris, Martin, 26, 27, 192n49
Hinckley, Gordon B., 20

Isaac, 117

Jacob, 105, 117
James (apostle), 19, 28, 29, 42, 75, 178
Jared, 84
Jesus, 19, 116–17, 143–44
John (apostle), 19, 28, 29, 42, 75, 159, 178
John the Baptist, 19, 28, 35, 42, 104

Kimball, Spencer W., 59, 105
Knight, Joseph, 27

Lehi, 84–85
Lincoln, Abraham, 56
Lucifer, 107, 108, 134

Lund, Anthon H., 101
Luther, Martin, 69–70

McConkie, Bruce, 9, 13, 46, 64, 66, 75, 80, 101, 106, 108, 111, 112, 117, 138, 140, 162, 165, 171, 196n34
Melchizedek, 28, 29, 38, 74, 75
Michael (archangel), 104, 107, 108, 172
Millet, Robert, 9, 12, 14, 70, 81, 102, 108, 116, 118, 127, 134, 137, 144, 163, 167, 200n39, 203n23
Mormon (Nephite prophet), 23, 86
Moroni, 19, 21–24, 27, 42, 86, 91, 104, 159, 191n31
Moses, 19, 33, 34, 42, 89
Mouw, Richard, 93
Muhammad, 88

Noah, 85, 104

Ostling, Richard and Joan, 14, 153

Page, Hiram, 34, 192n49
Partridge, Edward, 36
Paul (apostle), 115, 131, 137, 140, 141, 144, 147, 148

InDex of scripture